A SCRATCH MODELER'S LOG

BY HENRY BRIDENBECKER & A. RICHARD MANSIR

M'

A MOONRAKER PUBLICATION
BY AERO PUBLISHERS, INC.
FALLBROOK, CALIFORNIA

A Moonraker Publication
By
AERO PUBLISHERS
329 W. Aviation Road
Fallbrook, CA 92028

Library of Congress Cataloging
in Publication Data

Bridenbecker, Henry
and A. Richard Mansir
A scratch modeler's log.

"A Moonraker publication"—T.p. verso.
1. Ship models. I. Title.
VM298.B74 1984   623.8'201   24-12345
ISBN 0-8168-0014-6 (pbk.)

Copyright © 1984 by A. Richard Mansir. All Rights Reserved. Printed in the United States of America. No part of this publication may be reproduced, stored in a retrieval system, or transmitted, in any form or by any means, electronic, mechanical, photocopying, recording, or otherwise, without prior written permission.

PRINTED AND BOUND IN THE UNITED STATES OF AMERICA

ISBN 0-8168-0014-6

TABLE OF CONTENTS

INTRODUCTION	4
MALEK ADHEL, 1840	8
A SPANISH GALLEON OF 1540 AD	10
THE SHIP FROM KYRENIA CA 300 BC	14
THE SHIP FROM YASSI ADA, 7th CENTURY AD	19
A CARRACK OF THE 14TH CENTURY AD	23
THE SHIP FROM KALMAR, 13TH CENTURY AD	28
THE BRIG IRENE, 1806	33
THE THOLENSE HOOGAARS TH64, 1850	41
THE SAMBUC OF ARABIA	44
A CHINESE WAR JUNK, 19TH CENTURY	48
SHIP BUILDING IN COLONIAL AMERICA	52
THE VIRGINIA OF THE SAGADAHOCK	53
A COLONIAL BARK, 1640	56
THE HANNAH, A COLONIAL SCHOONER, 1775	58
A TANCOOK WHALER, 1900	64
SPRAY, CAPTAIN SOLCUM'S SLOOP 1895	69
A U.S. NAVY ANCHOR HOY, 1820	74
FANNY M, A PISCATAQUA RIVER GUNDALOW, 1886	77
THE BUILDING OF THE SHIP, LONGFELLOW	81
PART II: TIPS FOR THE MODELER	86
SOURCES OF PLANS AND OTHER DATA	111

INTRODUCTION

There is an old saying that says "necessity is the mother of invention," and I sincerely believe that it applies to scratch-building ship models. A scratchbuilder does not rely on ready-made products for his model, but makes them through his own effort and ingenuity from any raw material he may have on hand. If it is made carefully and to scale, his scratchbuilt hatch cover, lifeboat or capstan will be perfectly suited to the model under construction. This book is mainly about my own brand of scratchbuilding ingenuity and a view of the models that I have built with it over the years.

My interest in ship model building began in the middle 'twenties when I was about fourteen years of age. My modeling tools were few and simple. I had a block plane, knife, coping saw, ruler, a hand crank drill and my dad's big swivel vise. Glue was a problem at that time. We had Le Page liquid glue which was sticky but didn't hold wood very well. Then there was hot furniture glue which smelled to high heaven when it was heated on my mother's kitchen stove. Of course it didn't hold well unless the material being glued was clamped under pressure, and it took several hours to set up. It left a bit to be desired in model work. Nonetheless I persevered.

Scratchbuilding, as it is called today, was standard practice for me since, to me, kits and model plans didn't exist. Even if they had I would not have been able to afford them. My building material consisted of sugar pine, cedar from cigar boxes, and stiff brown cardboard from manila folders. Small cans of enamel in various colors were available at the five and ten cent store; they took forever to dry. Wire brads were the best fasteners, and very small screw eyes made fine deck ring bolts. My "plans" were pictures of small boats found in different magazines. I copied their lines as best I could to fashion a model. I thought the results of my labors were pretty good if the model roughly *resembled* a boat. Scale was something that formed inside of a teakettle.

Popular Science Magazine furnished me with my first ship model projects by supplying me with drawings and instructions for building various solid hull models. I remember one of my first models was of the old destroyer *Indianapolis* which I covered with several coats of battleship gray paint.

My next big project was building a Spanish Galleon from drawings by Capt. E. Armitage McCann. Captain McCann has been often called the "father" of modern model shipbuilding.

INTRODUCTION

He provided many fine articles on ship modeling years ago. I will never forget his advice on how to make deadeyes: You borrowed one of your mother's celluloid knitting needles and proceeded to slice off several thin discs. Next you borrowed one of her smaller steel sewing needles and held it with pliers in a flame on the kitchen stove burner until it became red hot. The next step was to burn three lanyard holes in the celluloid discs. My best score as I recall, was about three acceptable deadeyes out of ten.

I built two or three solid hull and bread-and-butter models under McCann's tutelage in that period, one of which was a Baltimore clipper. I worked six months of the year 1937 on this one, after which it experienced a fatal collision with a football. This was discouraging, but undismayed I moved on to my first true plank-on-frame model, the *Malek Adhel*.

Once again Captain McCann's *Popular Science* articles provided me the plans and the how-tos.

When I started making ship frames and cant frames, and fastening them to the keel and deadwood, fashioning bilge-stringers and beam shelves, and building up the many structural members of the hull, I became completely involved in this fascinating new dimension of the craft.

Unfortunately my hobby time was limited to a very few hours each week. Raising a family, home maintenance chores, and working every day took priority (as it should have) so it took me several years to complete *Malek Adhel*. But I knew the time would come when I could "plank-on-frame" to my heart's content, and it did.

After our children had grown up and left home, and while convalescing for over six months at the house with a fractured hip and pelvis, my hobby came really alive. With encouragement and much help from my wife, I assembled and rigged (while being held rigidly in a cast) several plastic models, and was finally able to finish the upper rigging on the *Malek Adhel*. My time to build model ships came during an enforced "vacation." As soon as it became economically possible, I retired from work and got into a full scale, 35 hour week of ship modeling. I still adhere to the routine.

The leisure time I now enjoy enables me to do some reading and research for each ship model project I undertake. This adds to the pleasure of the hobby because of the interesting facts

INTRODUCTION

to be learned about the evolution of ship building and the historical background of our seafaring forefathers, including pirates, slavers, and stout hearted fishermen.

Some of my peers think my choice of modeling subjects uncommon, if not a little strange. I search for a good set of plans of a ship not often built by modelers. For example, I have built a service boat, a river barge, an ancient coastal trader, a Dutch fisherman, and other not so famous or very grand vessels. But they played an important part in the development of shipping as the craft of the everyday people in our history. My models now span a period from 300 B.C. on into the latter part of the 19th century. Each model is of a different type and period, and has provided me with some special knowledge about its construction and function as well as something about the life style of the men who sailed on it.

I have discovered that about the best and easiest way to construct a ship model is to build it as closely as practicable to the way in which the real ship was assembled. It takes longer to build the model this way, but time, to me, is of little importance, since the enjoyment and satisfaction of building is what modeling is all about.

An authentically modelled ship fits together naturally. You don't have to fake the interior construction, and you can better appreciate and understand her structural beauty. Even if you decide to conceal the interior framing by completely planking the hull, you still know that the ship is honestly built and so rewards you with a feeling of pride in your work. That's why I always correct mistakes, however small. If ignored they tend to accumulate and finally, after a thousand hours of work, the model comes out spoiled in overall appearance.

Scale is of the utmost importance in building any model if it is to be a true replica. Nothing is more upsetting to me than to see a ship's ladder with steps two feet apart, belaying pins four feet long, or hatch grating openings large enough for a man to put his leg through. One reason for such scale discrepancies is the modeler's selection of parts and fittings from a ship model shop having a limited stock of ship's wheels, ladders, winches, hatch covers and anchors, which may or may not be of the correct scale size, or are too crudely made to be satisfactory. I scratch build the required fittings as much as I can. It takes longer, but I get exactly what I want while increasing my model-

INTRODUCTION

ing skill in the development of techniques.

Do I model everything down to the captain's pocket comb? No. My test is the smallest fixture or detail that can be distinguished with the naked eye if the model is assumed to be the real thing about 75 feet away. If an item is too small to identify at this distance, I don't attempt to make it. Its absence won't be missed, but it will certainly stand out if it is in place and out of scale.

Model scales I most commonly use are 1/8", 3/16", 1/4", and 3/8" equal to 1'–0". Larger scales are used for small vessels, smaller scales for large ships. This is so you have enough room to display them properly. About the smallest scale which will permit reasonably good detail is 1/4" equals 1'–0".

There are a large variety of woods available to ship modelers. The woods most preferred are those easy to work and hard enough to hold a sharp edge when cut into small thin "timbers." The grain should be fine enough to conform to scale. Oak for example is usually a poor choice because it is too coarse grained to look well, even though it was one of the primary woods used in real ship construction. Pine and balsa are too soft to hold the clean edges needed. On the other hand, I've used all of these materials on occasion.

I like to use California alder for a general purpose model wood. It is hard, has a look of oak, makes excellent frames and planks, and takes a pleasing natural golden finish. I also like poplar. This wood has a slightly greenish color. Both of these are in good supply and are not expensive. Swiss pear is a beautiful, dark brown wood and is fine for blocks and deadeyes as well as caprails and wales. Boxwood is ideal for making small blocks, very finely detailed deck fixtures such as winches, capstans, and ship wheels. But it is becoming a scarce wood and is comparatively expensive.

These are just some of the woods that I have had good results with, but there are many others I am sure would work equally well. I use woods for their distinctive shades and colors. I leave my models unpainted, and let the natural color of the woods provide pleasing color contrasts.

What follows here is a presentation of my models, most of them built since my retirement in 1975, and some of the techniques and construction methods I have worked out while solving the problems of the scratch ship modeler.

MALEK ADHEL, 1840

The *Malek Adhel* is a 1/4" = 1'–0" scale, plank-on-frame model of a merchant brig. I constructed this model with the aid of blueprints and written directions prepared by Capt. Armitage McCann for a 1937 series of Popular Science articles. I learned a great deal about *how not to build* a plank on frame model on this project. I cast aside a good number of structural parts that didn't meet Capt. McCann's ship modeling standards before I was done.

The frames, keel, stem and sternposts, keelson, and all of the hull planks were provided by a dining room table leaf of gumwood which was sliced into many strips of various thicknesses. The deck was made of narrow mahogany planks, and the masts and spars were of birch. The model was held together with white glue, and small 3/8-inch brass pins whose heads were later filed off. A shipyard type jig was erected which was similar to that described by C. G. Davis in his book, *The Built-Up Ship Model*, which held the frames erect and properly spaced while the keelson, bilge stringers, and wales were fastened in place.

I left a few planks off of the starboard side to display the ribs and interior construction. The bulwarks were painted black outside, and white inside. The waterways were blue and the masts, bowsprit, and tops were white as were the bitts, fiferails, and the lifeboat. The rest of the ship was left unpainted but was given a few coats of clear satin finish lacquer well rubbed down. I started building this little brig in 1940 and finished it about thirty years later!

The designer and builder of the brig was the famous clipper ship builder, William H. Webb. He built the *Malek Adhel* for his own account, describing her as a "handsome and fast sailer." He planned to use her in the Pacific trades, but he may also have built her to prove his design ideas which, in the decade following *Malek Adhel*'s launch, gave rise to some of the fastest sailing ships ever. Among these were the *Flying Dutchman* and the *Young American*.

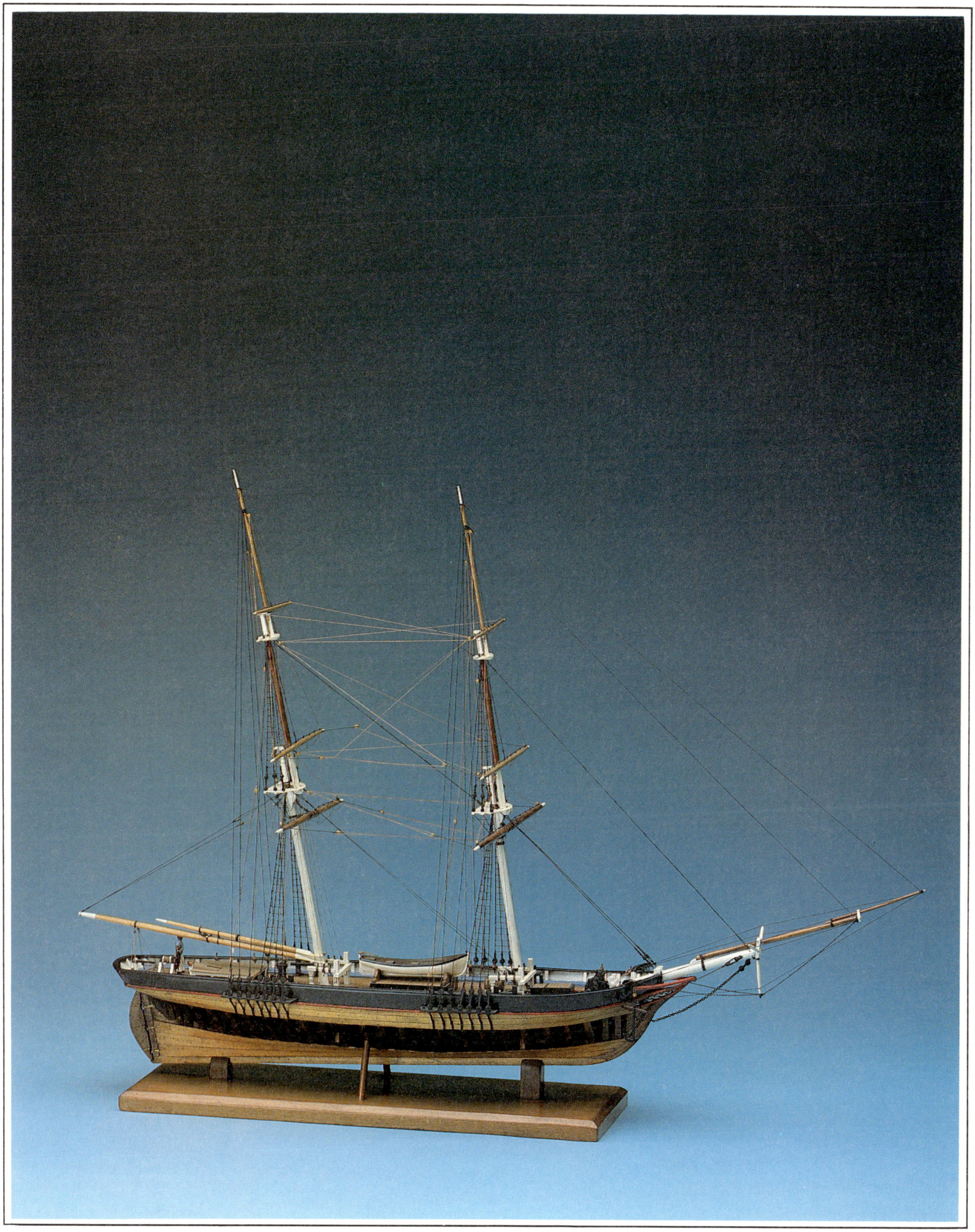

A SPANISH GALLEON OF 1540 AD

When I retired in 1975 my friends gave me a Billing kit of this Spanish galleon. The kit consisted of a simple set of plans, a stack of mahogany strips, several pre-cut plywood bulkheads, and a plywood cut-out of a keel, sternpost and stempost. Also included were sheets of thin plywood with black lines drawn on them to represent deck planks, doorways, and the fore and aft structures. A number of brass cannons and belaying pins were furnished, a quantity of sail cloth, rigging thread, small nails, colored plastic strips for making the round fighting tops, and plastic deadeyes and blocks. The building instructions were translated into English from Swedish. They left a great deal to be desired.

This galleon is the only kit model I have in my collection, all the rest are scratchbuilt. I don't care much for plywood as a building material, and plastic blocks and deadeyes have an unpleasant tendency to come apart under stress. I modified the model's structure. I built up the sterncastle, forecastle, and the decks with individual planks. I used bamboo dowels instead of nails to fasten the hull planking. The rigging drawings seemed fairly accurate so I used them. The net effect of the model as I finally completed her seems to be reasonably representative of a Spanish galleon of the period as far as historical records show.

This venture into kit model construction convinced me that scratch building and plank-on-frame construction was really the way I wanted to go. I decided that if I were going to spend many hours building a ship model it should be built as nearly as possible to the way the ship was actually constructed, rather than to use substitute methods such as plywood bulkheads and plastic fittings. But it took about ninety hours to build this kit model. Had I built her from scratch from a detailed set of plans, it would probably have taken five hundred hours to complete. Clearly, kits have their place.

The flag of Spain bears the armorials of the kingdoms of Castile (castle) and Leon (lion). Unified in the thirteenth century, Castile and Leon exercised sovereignty over nearly all the lesser kingdoms of medieval Spain. The power of the unified kingdoms by the end of the fifteenth century, extended over all of Spain, to Italy, France and to the new lands of America.

There are plenty of beautifully built kit models around, hardly inferior to my pet scratch-built efforts. Newcomers to shipmodeling are well advised to start with a small kit model, working on to more complex projects. They will learn much about rigging, hull shapes, ship fittings, and ship terms, which could prepare them for scratch building later on.

This "Spanish Galleon" of the period around 1540 is essentially the sort of ship that made up the great "Armada" of 1588, and also played a large role in the building of Spain's colonial empire in the 16th century. Galleons, direct descendents of the earlier carracks, were huge by contemporary standards, some of them as large as 1800 tons. My model is of a ship about 70' on deck and perhaps 100 tons burthen, and so is a comparatively small "nao," as the Spanish called a merchant ship.

SPANISH GALLEON
CA1540 AD
Length app. 70′ O.A
Beam app. 22′
Tonnage app. 100

13

THE SHIP FROM KYRENIA CA 300 BC

The wreck of this vessel was recovered from the Mediterranean Sea in 1969 by underwater archaeologist, George Bass. The ship was found off the north coast of Cyprus near the town of Kyrenia.

Carbon 14 tests on her hull planks show that she was built around 370 BC. The same test on some almonds included in her cargo indicate that she sank in 288 BC. The little ship lived an astonishing 84 years, overlapping the career of Alexander the Great (336 BC–323 BC).

During her lifetime Greece, as a unified political empire under Alexander, decayed into a complicated array of 100 city states, three monarchies, and endless dozens of political alliances and leagues that came and went as individuals angled for power in the period scholars call the "Hellenistic" era.

But in spite of the political mess Greek commerce, culture and science flourished all over the ancient world. In Alexandria, Egypt, Euclid wrote his famous "Elements" of geometry om 300 BC; Archimedes earned fame in Syracuse; and in 306 BC, Epicurus, the old philosopher of easy living, opened his school in Athens.

The wealth that supported the Hellenistic good life derived from a virile international trade. Goods flowed to and fro from China to Spain through great Greek trading cities such as Babylon, Rhodes, Corinth, Syracuse, Carthage, Rome and hundreds more.

Ships played an important role in all this commerce and many were built to substantial size, up to 200 feet in length. Navigation of the open seas was a matter of course, and vessels made passages averaging a healthy six knots per hour.

The evidence of the cargo aboard the ship from Kyrenia suggests that she was trading southwards along the Turkish/Anatolian coast, making ports on the islands of Samos, Kos, and Rhodes.

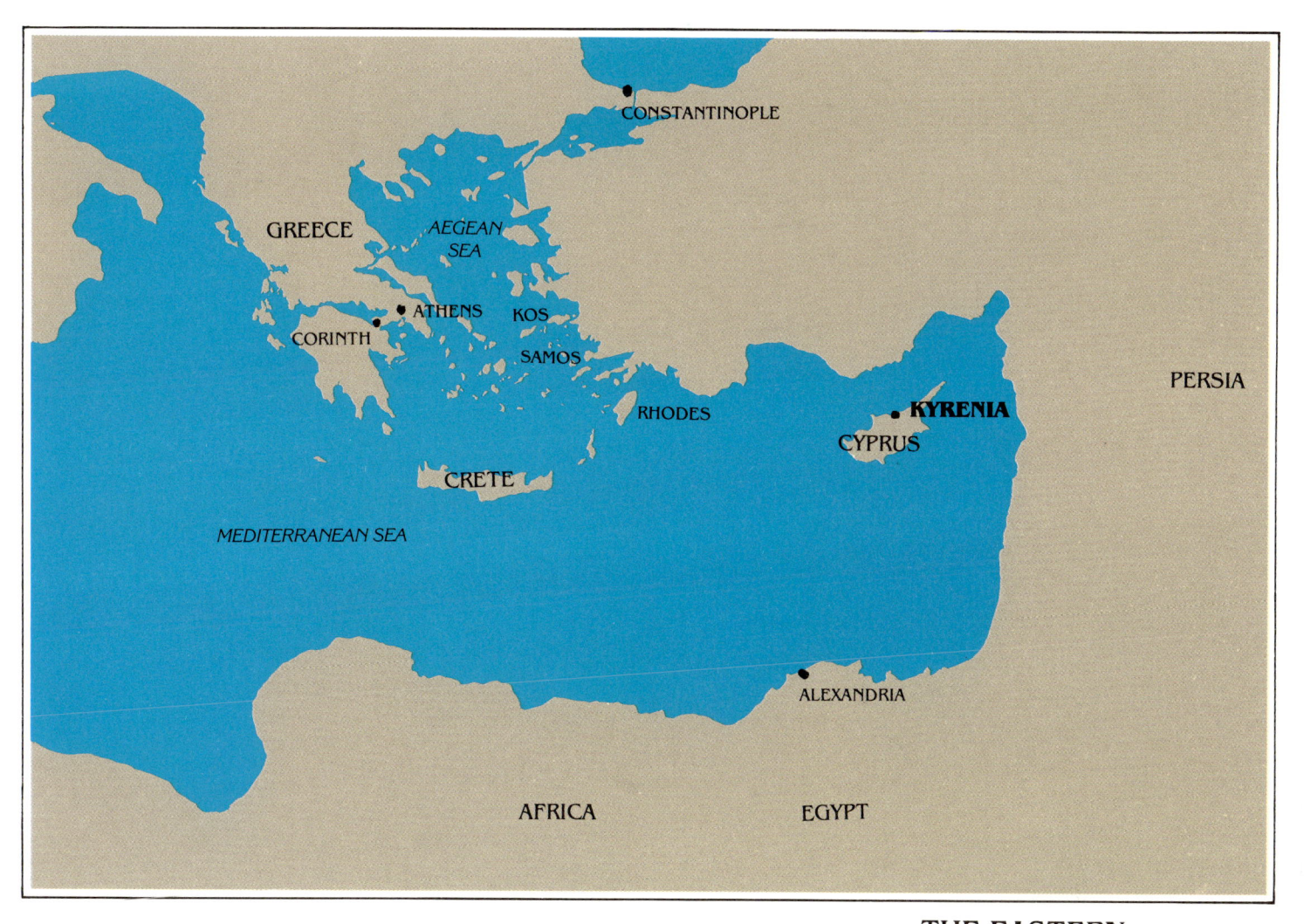

THE EASTERN MEDITERRANEAN

She was 47 feet long, 14½ feet wide, and had been built shell first, the method I used in building the model. The ship was built carvel fashion with the planks edge joined together with mortis and tenon fastenings. After the shell was built it was strengthened with small ribs nailed to the planks. It was further reinforced by a few transverse through-beams and two pairs of heavy wales. Weather cloths of woven matting (my wife wove some for the model) were fastened to wooden stanchions to keep the ocean spray from wetting the cargo. The cap rails were only about two feet above the water.

She was guided by port and starboard steering oars, and was propelled by a single wide, square sail, raised and lowered by a number of brail ropes. The speed of the coaster, estimated at four to five knots, was controlled by the amount of sail area exposed to the wind.

The Ship from Kyrenia
Length O.A.—47'-0"
Beam—14'-6"
Model Scale—3/8"=1'-0"

The model was constructed from an artist's drawing in the November 1974 *National Geographic,* and from various photos of the recovered wreck. I determined some of the sizes of the beams and planks from a photo of a workman's fist on one of the beams. The average size of a fist across the knuckles is about four inches. With the assistance of proportional dividers I drew plans and line drawings for a mold over which the hull was constructed.

The planks were made of straight grained redwood. I made the beams, ribs, and rails of fruitwood obtained from a dismantled davenport. I discovered that redwood, though beautiful in color, is not satisfactory for modeling. It is too soft and brittle, and is easily dented. The Kyrenia was held together with small bamboo dowels, and "Tight-Bond" glue. I left it unpainted but gave it several coats of satin finish lacquer rubbed down between coats.

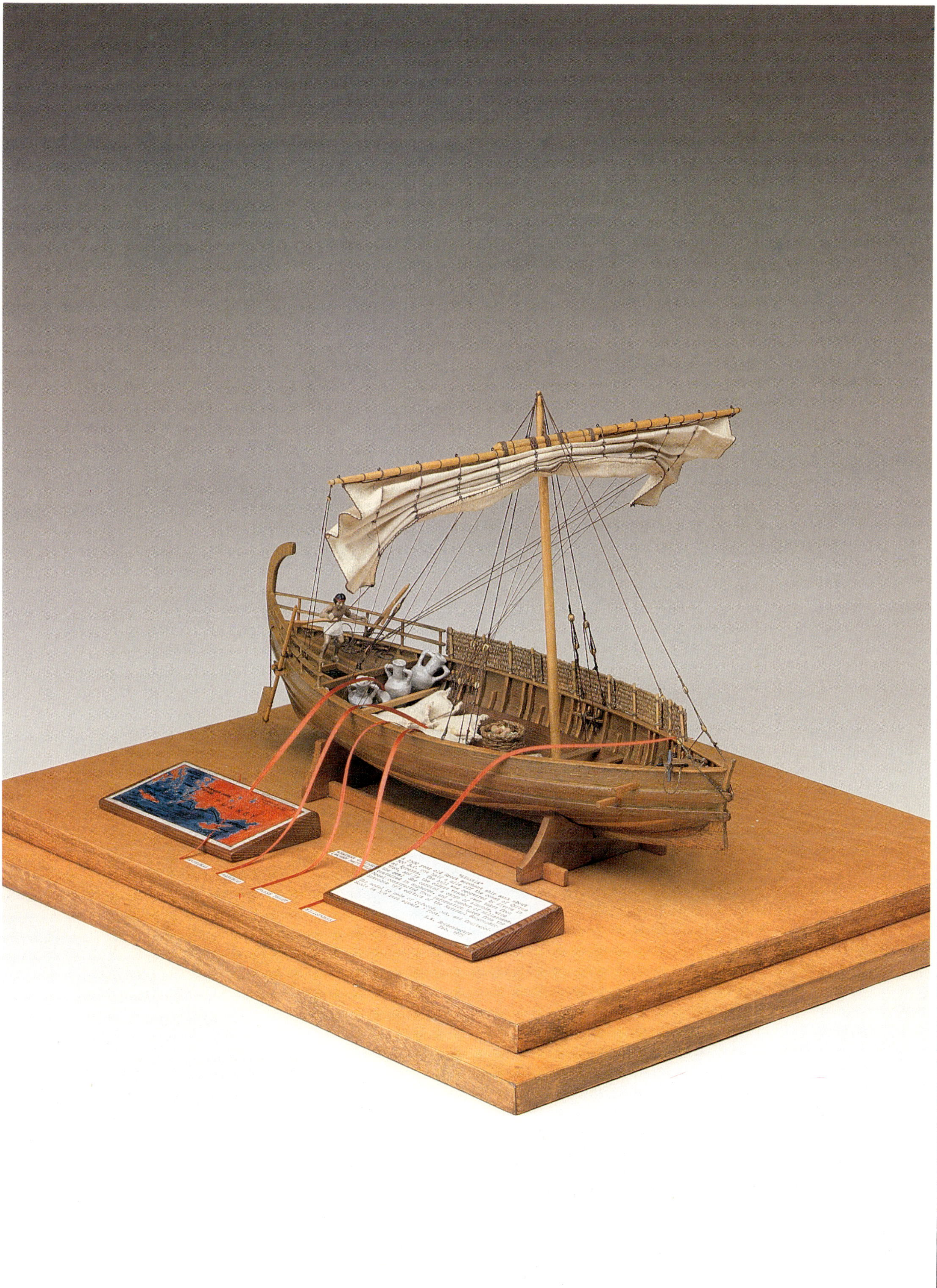

The cargo of the ship from Kyrenia consisted of almonds, and over 400 wine amphorae. I only included five amphorae in my model to convey the idea. She also carried 29 stone grain-mills (to the left in the photo) stowed along the axis of the keel for ballast.

The rigging of the ship from Kyrenia, of course, had all rotted away when she was recovered, except that a block was found near her mast step. The model is rigged in accordance with what is known about the rigs of all Greek ships of her time, particularly the famous triremes.

This small merchant ship dates from the 7th century A.D. She was recovered also by George Bass and his team in 1961 near the little island of Yassi Ada (flatrock) in the eastern Aegean. Yassi Ada lies just offshore from the Turkish mainland not far from the ancient city of Halicarnassus, home of Heroditus (today Badrum). The island of Kos lies just to the south. The ship traded on the same coast as the Kyrenian vessel.

The ship from Yassi Ada spent her days serving a troubled Byzantine Empire. In the 7th century the country once ruled by the emperor Justinian was under attack from Persia to the east, barbarian tribes to the north, and Moslem hordes from the east and south. Only a stout general and emperor, Heraclius, managed to keep Constantinople Greek.

But even in the midst of war, trade went on, and shipowners like Georgios, who owned this ship, dared the piracy and hostility of their world to earn a living at sea.

The ship from Yassi Ada was 62 feet long and 17 wide. She sank in 120 feet of water with a cargo of about 900 amphorae of wine in her.

The hull planking was loosely edge joined together up to the water line, then heavy frames were attached to the keel. The planks were then fastened to the frames with iron nails. Four pairs of half timbers served as wales girding the upper sides of the hull and were bolted to the frames. There were two through beams amidship supporting the mast and two more projected outboard near the stern which supported port and starboard steering oars. The ship was built from cyprus, elm and pine, and all fastenings were of iron.

THE SHIP FROM YASSI ADA, 7TH CENTURY AD

The Ship from Yassi Ada
Length—62'-0"
Beam—17'-0"
Model Scale—1/36

21

The major sphere of influence of the Byzantine Empire at its height

The use of thinner planking over heavy frames provided a much stronger hull and probably marked the beginning of plank-on-frame carvel construction. Economic considerations seem to have fostered this new method of construction.

There was a tile roof slightly over two feet above the deck at the stern which covered the galley. The cooking was done on a tile hearth suspended on clay-embedded iron bars which reduced the fire hazard. Fire was a real danger in old wooden ships.

My model was made from lines drawings developed from on-site measurements by archaeologists. They were reproduced in G. Bass' book on underwater archaeology. I picked up additional details from a *National Geographic* article.

I used proportional dividers to enlarge the drawings to a scale of 1"=3'–0" and to lay out the proportions of the 30 planks covering each side of the hull's 53 frames.

T housands of carracks, large and small, plied the Mediterranean in the 14th century. They were the seagoing work horses of the Middle Ages and many of them were owned by the merchants of the Italian city states. The Italians, particularly the Venetians, grew rich on the trade between Byzantium and the East, and the new markets of western Europe. The wealth generated by the carracks spurred on the Italian Renaissance—a passion for learning and cultural development—which had just begun to take hold when this little carrack was built.

My model is of a ship 64'-9" long, 22'-5" wide with a burthen of perhaps 75 tons. Other carracks of the time were monsters of 1500 or more tons burthen.

Italy, at the time my carrack lived, was a lusty, booming place. Venice alone had 3,300 ships for war or trade and 36,000 seamen to man them. Genoa, the home of Christopher Columbus, and arch rival of Venice, dominated nearly as many trade routes and as many ducats.

Among the famous names of the time and place were Dante Alighieri writing his Divine Comedy; Simone Boccanera, commemorated by Verdi in his opera about him, was leading a popular revolt to become the first of the Genoese Boccanera doges; and the painter Giotto was making the famous decorations of the Arena Chapel in Padua; Boccaccio was writing his Decameron; and finally a fellow by the name of Frencesco di Petracco was wandering about making notes for some of the most famous poetry in history.

A CARRACK OF THE 14TH CENTURY AD

A Carrack of the 14th Century
Length—64′-9″
Beam—22′-5″
Model Scale—3/16″=1′-0″

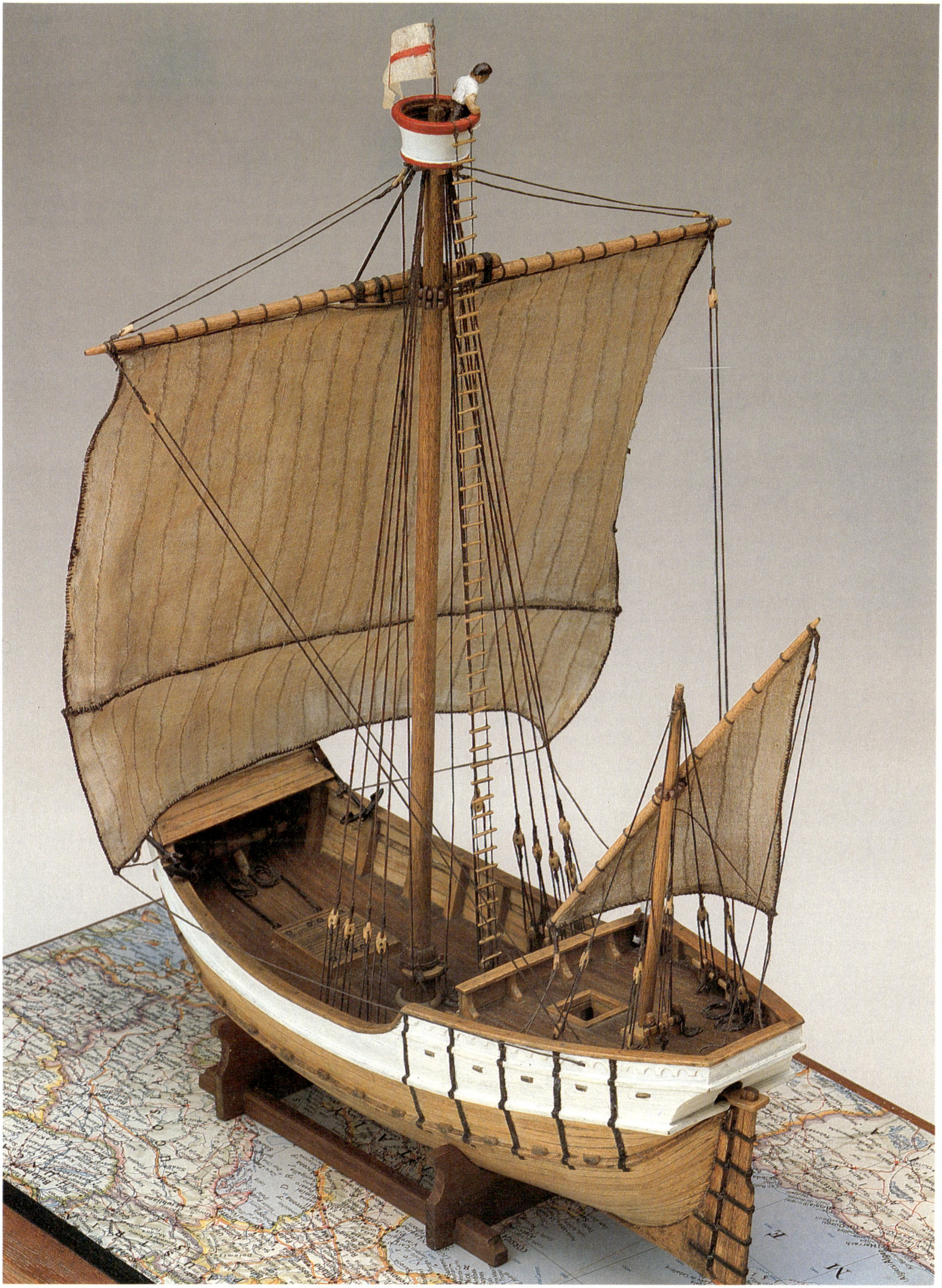

The flag of Venice symbolizes the city's location between the sea and the land and its vision of itself as the guardian of maritime endeavor.

Francesco di Petracco lived between 1304 and 1374 and became known to the world as Petrarch. Petrarch recorded the life and times of Italy in the 14th century, and in so doing earned himself the title of "Father of the Italian Renaissance."

For a time Petrarch lived in Venice. He described the shipping like this: "I see vessels . . . as big as my mansion, their masts taller than its towers, they are as mountains floating on the waters. They go to face incalculable dangers in every portion of the globe. They bear wine to England, honey to Russia, saffron, oil and linen to Assyria, Armenia, Persia, and Araby, wood to Egypt and Greece. They return heavily laden with products of all kinds which are sent hence to every part of the world."

My carrack is carvel built with a stern rudder, an innovation of the time. It has a fore and after castle, and the decks are all supported with through beams. The mast had a top which was reached by a long rope ladder, and the shrouds were rigged with long tackles. It had a main square sail and a small lateen sail at the stern to aid in steering.

I made the model from a painting by Landstrom in *The Ship*. There were no given dimensions, but human figures in the drawing (average height of a man about 5 ft. 8 in.) gave me a scale to work with. Using an old shipbuilders formula of "1–2–3" meaning length three times the breadth and keel twice the breadth, I made a set of lines drawings.

My model is to a scale of 3/16"=1'–0".

This painting of a carrack was copied from a much larger painting made in Venice in 1495 by Vittore Carpaccio. Carpaccio's painting, one of several romantic panoramas of Venetian life by the old master, includes views of a half dozen such ships along a bustling Venetian waterfront. The title of Carpaccio's painting is "The Bride and Bridegroom Taking Leave of Their Parents."

THE SHIP FROM KALMAR, 13TH CENTURY AD

When this ship was built the Baltic Sea trade was dominated by the Hanseatic League. The Hanseatic League was a loose confederation of towns situated on the shores of the Baltic and the North Sea. The confederation was an economic one designed to control the commerce of northwestern Europe.

The original towns were German maritime towns—Lubeck, Hamburg, Luneburg, Wismar, Rostock and Stralsund. Later Scandinavian towns, particularly on the island of Gotland, were added as were "counting centers" in Flanders and England.

At a time when the general political organization of Europe was weak and decentralized, the League exerted enormous power and prestige. It patrolled the Baltic against pirates, made and enforced laws on matters of trade, regulated the disposition of shipwrecked goods, and decided absolutely who and who would not conduct business in their very wide sphere of influence. They ran banks, set up any number of sophisticated financial systems, introduced a system of standard weights and measures, and maintained a maritime intelligence network. They also built and maintained canals, harbor facilities, shipyards and shoreside warehouses.

Merchants desiring to trade in a given hanse town paid dues, while the League as a whole continued to press for exclusive trading privileges in more and more communities.

The Hanseatic League reached the height of its influence in the 14th century, 100 years after the ship from Kalmar was launched. But there is little doubt that this little vessel was owned and operated by members of a hansa.

Kalmar is located along the southeast coast of Sweden on the mainland side of Kalmar Sound. Across the sound is the Island of Oland.

The remains of the ship from Kalmar were discovered in 1933 while Kalmar harbor was being dredged.

SPHERE OF INFLUENCE OF THE HANSEATIC LEAGUE

The vessel was 36½ feet long and 15 feet wide. It was clinker built of oak, and the ribs were riveted to the planking instead of being bound to cleats as in the case of earlier Viking ships. The coaster was built shell first; thirteen planks to a side with small ribs added to stiffen the hull. Through beams were installed fore and aft and amidships for greater hull strength, and were further joined to the planking with knees. A rudder was attached to a straight stern post, a recent innovation in steering gear at the time. A windlass aided in hoisting the sail and raising and lowering the mast. The mast could be lowered easily by removing a short crosspiece held in place by wooden pins from the mast partners.

The Ship from Kalmar
Length—36'-6"
Beam—15'-0"
Model Scale—3/8"=1'-0"

My model was constructed mainly from a sketch in Landstrum's book, *The Ship*, showing the vessel beached on the sand with the yard and sail lowered. I also referred to photographs and information about the recovered wreck in the book, *A History of Seafaring*, by George Bass; and from *Ships and the Sea*, by Duncan Haws.

I made drawings of the ship to a scale of 3/8"=1'–0", using proportional dividers and overall dimensions given by Landstrom.

I formed the hull over a balsa wood mold. I inserted the knees, decks and through beams after the shell was removed from the mold. "Rivets" of bamboo dowels, painted black, were used to fasten the clinker planking. The model is made of gumwood, white oak, and alder. The sand and driftwood ladder came from Gold Beach, Oregon.

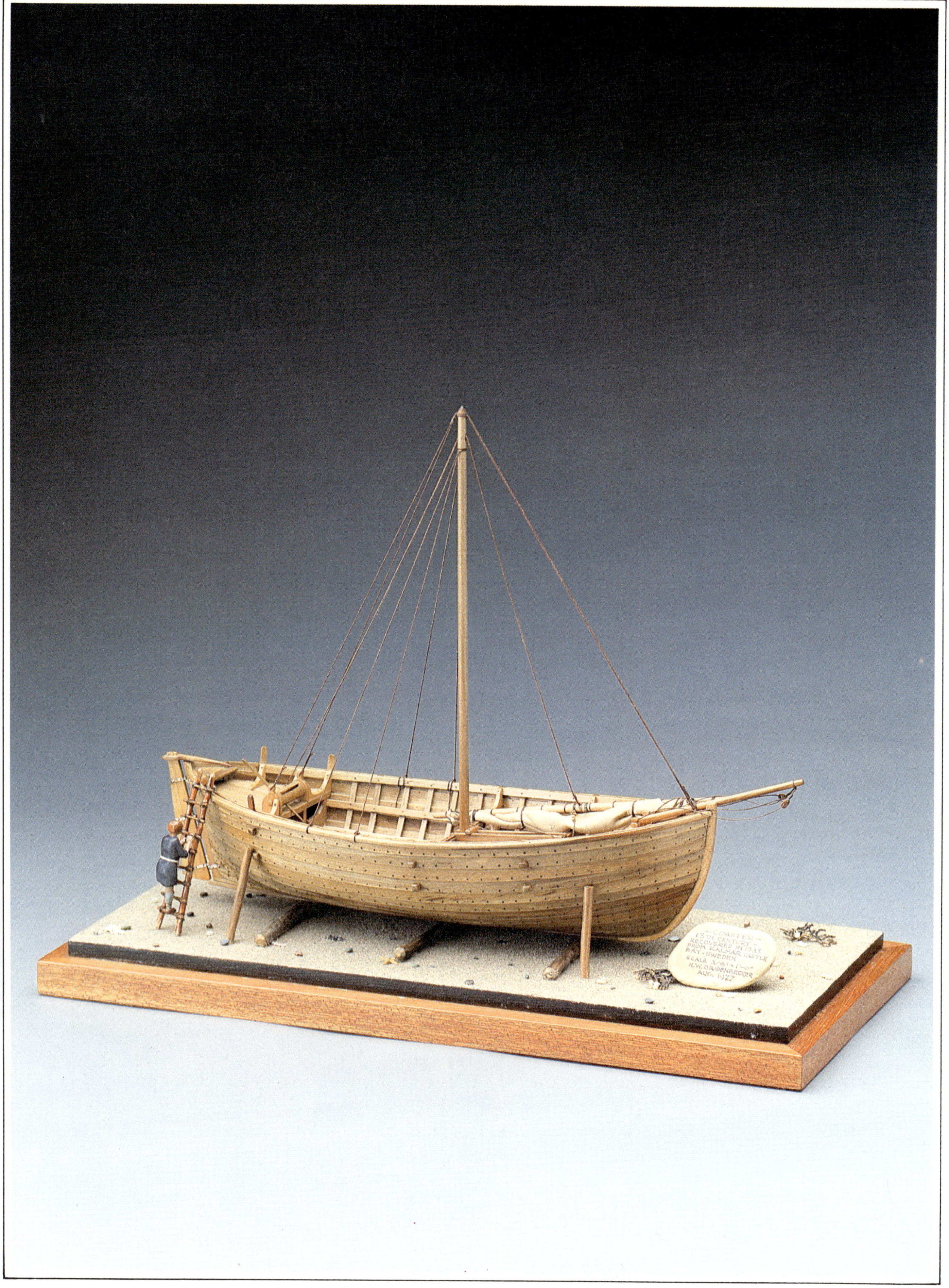

The view, looking aft toward the quarter deck, shows the windlass used for raising the mast as well as the large number of knees and throughbeams included in her structure. The ship from Kalmar also exhibits one of the earliest uses of a stern rudder.

The ship from Kalmar was a clinker-built in keeping with the ship building technology of the Vikings and other northerners. As the shell of the boat was built up with overlapping plank strakes, reinforcing ribs and knees were added.

THE BRIG IRENE, 1806

The 18 gun Dutch brig-of-war *Irene* was built in 1806 at Hythe, England, as H.M.S. *Grasshopper*. At the time, Napoleon Bonaparte was at the height of his career even though Nelson had decimated his fleet at Trafalgar the year before. *Grasshopper* actively served in the British navy until a violent storm off the Dutch coast caused her and two other ships to become stranded on dangerous sand banks. The two other ships broke up and were lost, but *Grasshopper* managed to float off the sand only to surrender to Napoleon's Dutch on Christmas Day, 1811. Her name was subsequently changed to *Irene*, and she became a member of the Dutch fleet.

The same year that *Grasshopper* was launched in England, 1806, Napoleon appointed his brother, Louis, King of Holland. Napoleon expected Louis to run Holland as Napoleon wished it to be run, but Louis had different ideas.

Napoleon's France and England were absolutely at war, and Napoleon had set up a Continental blockade against British goods and commerce. But Holland depended on British trade for its own economic health, and the enterprising Hollanders started a bootleg commerce with the English. Louis, more in sympathy with the Dutch than his brother, refused to prosecute the bootleggers. This irritated Napoleon so in 1810 he finally kicked Louis off his throne and annexed Holland to France. The following year French-Holland annexed *Grasshopper* and made her *Irene*.

Nominally Holland was England's enemy, but in fact was her ally. When the Duke of Wellington defeated Napoleon's "Armee du Nord" at Waterloo in 1815, a substantial number of his 93,000 troops were Dutchmen.

Irene's career in the Dutch navy ran parallel with the decline of Napoleon's, and so never saw action against her British builders. One can imagine *Irene* passing from a quiet service about the time Napoleon Bonaparte died on the island of St. Helena in the South Atlantic, May 5, 1821.

Under Napoleon the Dutch tri-color flag was modified to include a picture of 'Liberty' in the first canton. This flag, known as the flag of the *Batavian Republic,* was flown roughly from 1790 to 1814.

The Brig Irene
Length—100'-0"
Beam—30'-6 1/2"
Draft—10'-0"
Model Scale 1/4"=1'-0"

35

View of *Irene's* starboard quarter shows her jolly boat slung in the stern davits and her armament of carronades run out ready to fire. *Irene's* gunports except for the two "bridle ports" at the bow, had no port covers. In heavy weather the gunports would be closed with panels like hatch covers from inboard.

View of the deck amidship shows the detail at the foot of the mainmast, and the ship's launch bowsed to ringbolts in the deck. Just under the rail to the left and right can be seen the sheaves for the fore braces and jib sheets.

Grasshopper/Irene was 100′ long, 30′–6½″ in beam, and had a draft of 10′–0″.

My model of *Irene* was built from the comprehensive plans and data contained in E. W. Petrejus' book *Irene—A Handbook for the Building of Historic Ship Models*. Mr. Petrejus had been the curator of the Prinz Hendrik Museum in Rotterdam and is a renowned authority on the history of ship building.

"Irene" was certainly the most ambitious of my ship modeling projects so far. She took nearly 3,000 hours to build over a period of eighteen months.

I started her, as usual, by drafting out the frames and their spacing after which I could no longer even think about the hull. I turned to making the capstan. I shaped 26 pieces of Swiss pear for this one fitting. Then I built the 12-oared ships launch. This was a full scale modeling project in itself.

Finally I turned my attention once again to the hull itself and slowly built up each of the 35 frames. Each of these consisted of a dozen separate pieces of contrasting colored wood.

When I focused on the 16, 32 pounder carronades and two long guns I would have preferred to buy them. But, alas, the hobby shops were bare. I turned all the guns on a lathe out of birch using a template made from a hacksaw blade. My wooden guns once painted a flat, metallic black, convinced even the beady eyed they were honest iron.

Time passed and thousands of dowels and small pieces passed through my fingers until *Irene* complete with all her fittings and rigging looked properly finished.

I couldn't stand it. I went on and built a midship section of a contemporary warship, USN *Wasp* of 1803, and a vignette of one of *Irene*'s carronades. One cannot spend a year and a half on a project and just quit without some withdrawal symptoms.

Here are the woods I used in *Irene*: two shades of poplar for the frames and hull planking; holly decks; Swiss pear, birch, walnut, box, and alder for deck fittings, blocks, spars and other components.

The wood finish was rubbed out acrylic lacquer. Metal parts were blackened brass.

This model of the midship section of the USN sloop-of-war *Wasp,* 1803 displays the major structural components of ships like *Irene* in scale. One gets a sense of the massiveness of the timbers when comparing them to the scale figures in the model. For example, the distance from the bottom of the keel to the top of the keelson is as high as the man—nearly six feet of solid timber.

The carronade was a weapons innovation of the 18th century and came into use by the British navy in 1779. The carronade was a comparatively light weight gun using a smaller powder charge than a cannon firing a similar weight ball. The carronade's muzzle velocity was less and its barrel shorter than that of a cannon. The slower moving shot of the carronade shattered instead of piercing, its targets and took casualties aboard enemy vessels with a shower of lethal, wooden shrapnel.

Irene as she might have looked at anchor off the Dutch coast sometime in her career.

THE THOLENSE HOOGAARS TH64, 1850 AD

This Dutch fishing vessel fished the North Sea tidewaters of the province of Zeeland. Boats of her type could be seen at work well into the twentieth century. She was a shallow draft, flat bottomed sailing craft equipped with leeboards. She was 44 feet long with a beam at the mast of 13'–2". Her depth was 5'–7" at the mast, but she was deepest at the intersection of the stem and the bottom. This feature made it easier to get the boat off a shoal.

The lower sides consisted of three, 2 inch thick, lapstrakes plus a pair of rubbing strakes, which kept the water from climbing aboard. Above the rubbing strakes the carvel planked sides had an exaggerated tumble-home. The frame sections resembled a six-sided box beam providing great strength with a relatively small amount of wood.

The forward compartment contained a small stove for boiling shrimp as it was caught.

The gaff rigged main sail and the jib were loose footed. The outer jib, used in light airs, set on a retractable jib-boom.

My model was built to a scale of 1/4" = 1'–0". I built her over a series of 15 template molds mounted upside down on the baseboard. The templates matched the stations of the body plan. Once the planking was built-up, I removed the templates and fitted the frames and breasthooks. My "nails" were made of .0135" wire. I made every structural member shown in the plans, so my model is built in almost every detail like the real boat.

The plans for this model appeared in the June 1976 issue of the *Nautical Research Journal*. They had been prepared by Mr. J. van Betan, curator of the National Ship Museum in Antwerp, Belgium.

The hull planks are poplar, the decks willow, and the frames, leeboards and rudder are made from alder. The spars are birch.

Tholense Hoogaars TH68
Length—44'-0"
Beam—13'-2"
Depth at Mast—5'-7"
Model Scale—1/4"=1'-0"

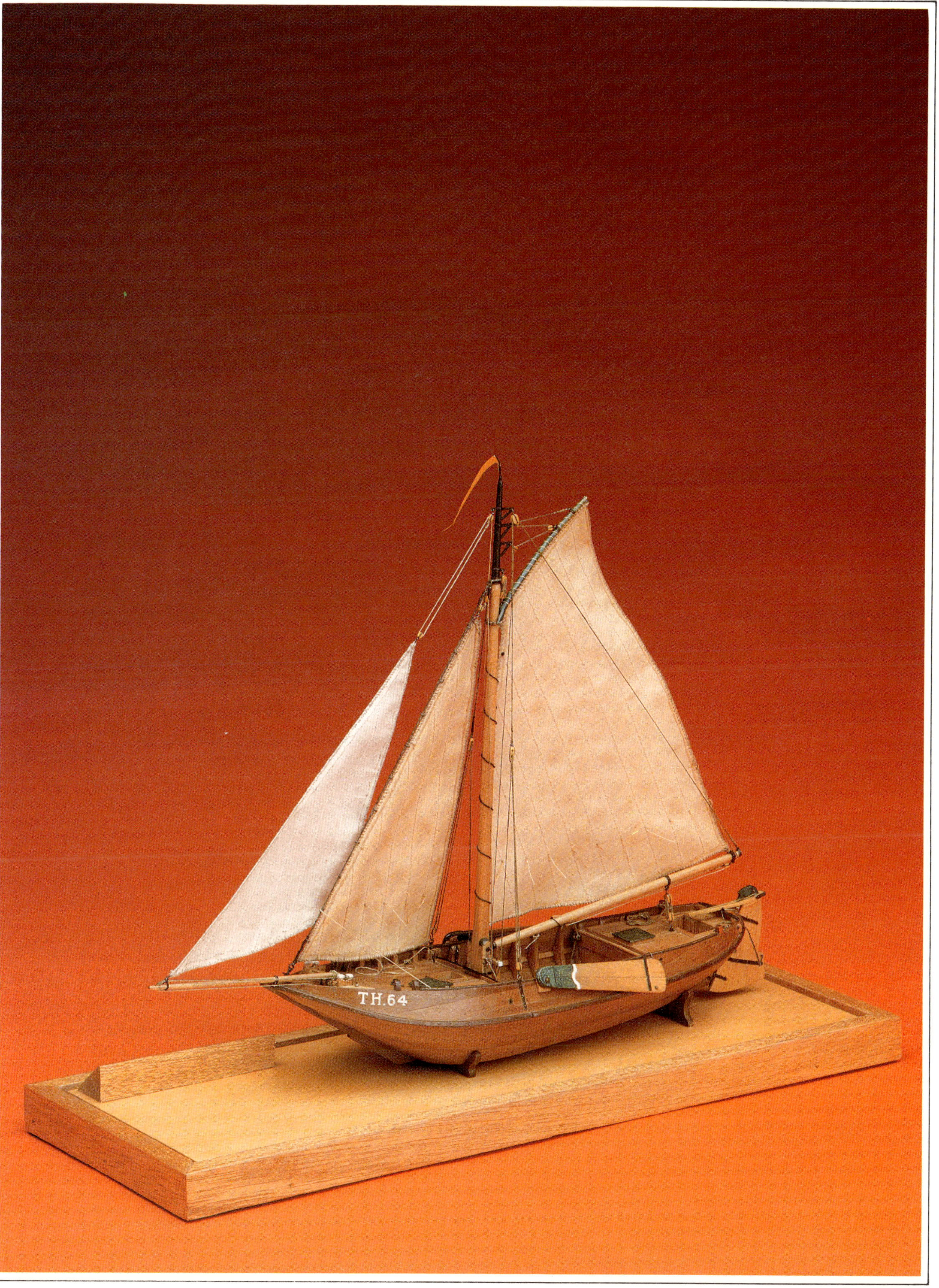
TH.64

THE SAMBUC OF ARABIA

The term "dhow" is a general term for any "cargo ship" in near eastern waters. My dhow was of a sort called a *sambuc*.

The inspiration for this project derived from Captain Alan Villiers' account of his year long voyage on a "boom," a larger type of dhow, down the coast of Africa to Zanzibar and back.

The dhows of the Near East reflect a basic design that has remained essentially unchanged since the time of Christ. The hull shape of the dhows is remarkably efficient, bearing a resemblance to that of the clipper ships designed 1800 years later.

The Arabs built their dhows planks first. They would plank the hull up a few strakes, then fit reinforcing ribs of tree branches, add a few more strakes, then more ribs and so on until the hull was complete. The ribs were placed where the builder felt they were needed.

The dhows carried a lateen rig—large triangular sails carried on long diagonal yards. The lateen rig is the earliest forerunner of the later fore and aft rigs. The Europeans started using lateen sails in the fifteenth century and continued to carry lateen mizzen sails well into the eighteenth century. The rig was very efficient.

Each of the long yards on a dhow consisted of two poles lashed together at the center. The yard could be lengthened or shortened depending on the size of sail needed. There was no reefing, just a collection of larger and smaller sails.

The mast shrouds were set up only on the windward side of a mast. When the ship came about, the shrouds were unhooked and shifted over to the opposite side.

My model is to a scale of 1/4" = 1'0" from a set of plans prepared by Vincenzo Lusci. I supplemented the plans with information gleaned from Captain Villiers' *Sons of Sinbad*.

I did not try to duplicate Arab ship building practice with this project. I built her hull plank-on-bulkhead fashion.

Arab dhows carried the trade goods of the Near East, over the Red Sea, Persian Gulf and Indian Ocean as far as Southern India, Ceylon, and South Africa. For years slaving was a major Arabian business in which dhows played a large role.

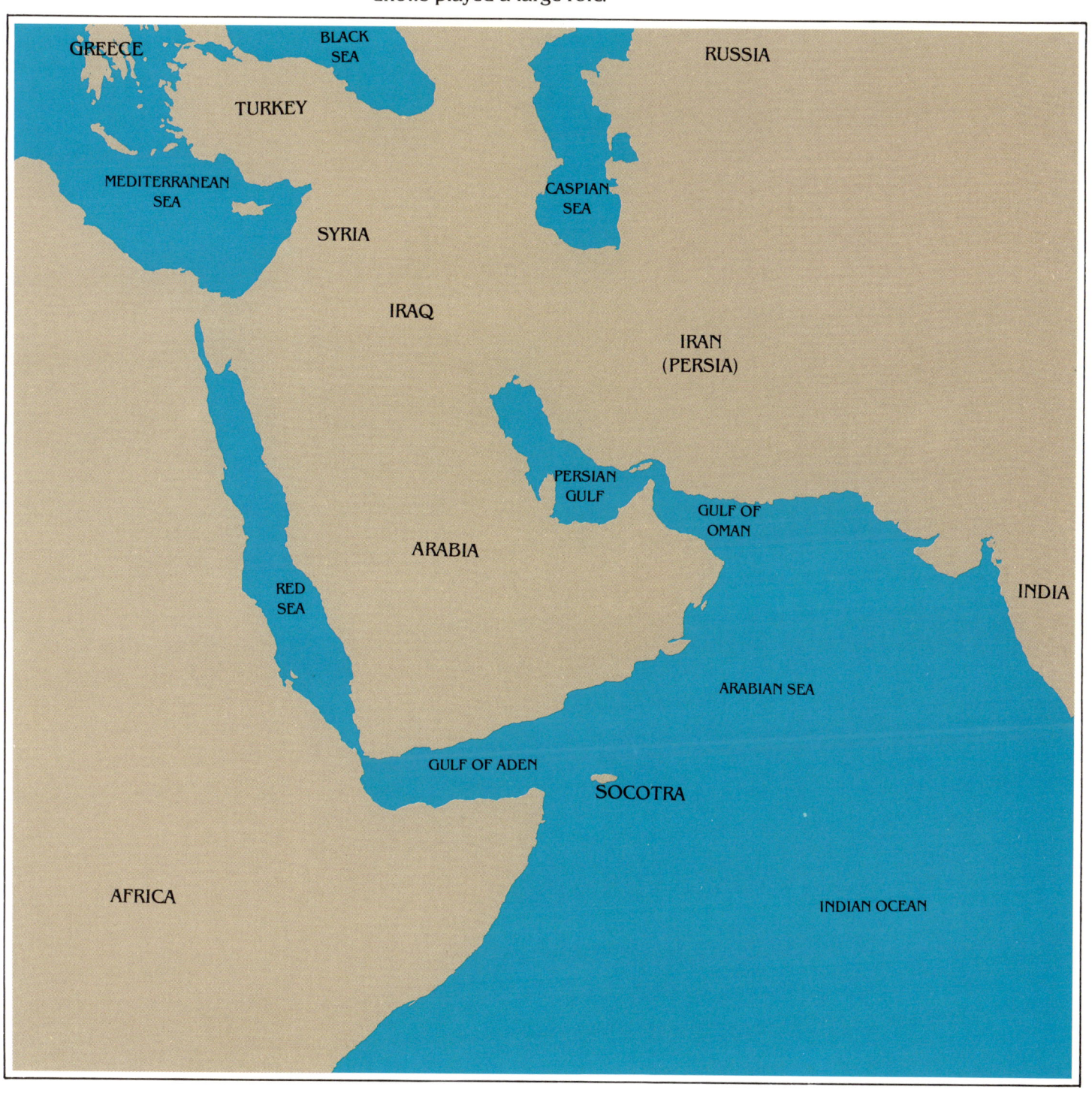

A Sambuc of Arabia
Length 70′
Beam 18′
Model Scale—1/4″=1′-0″

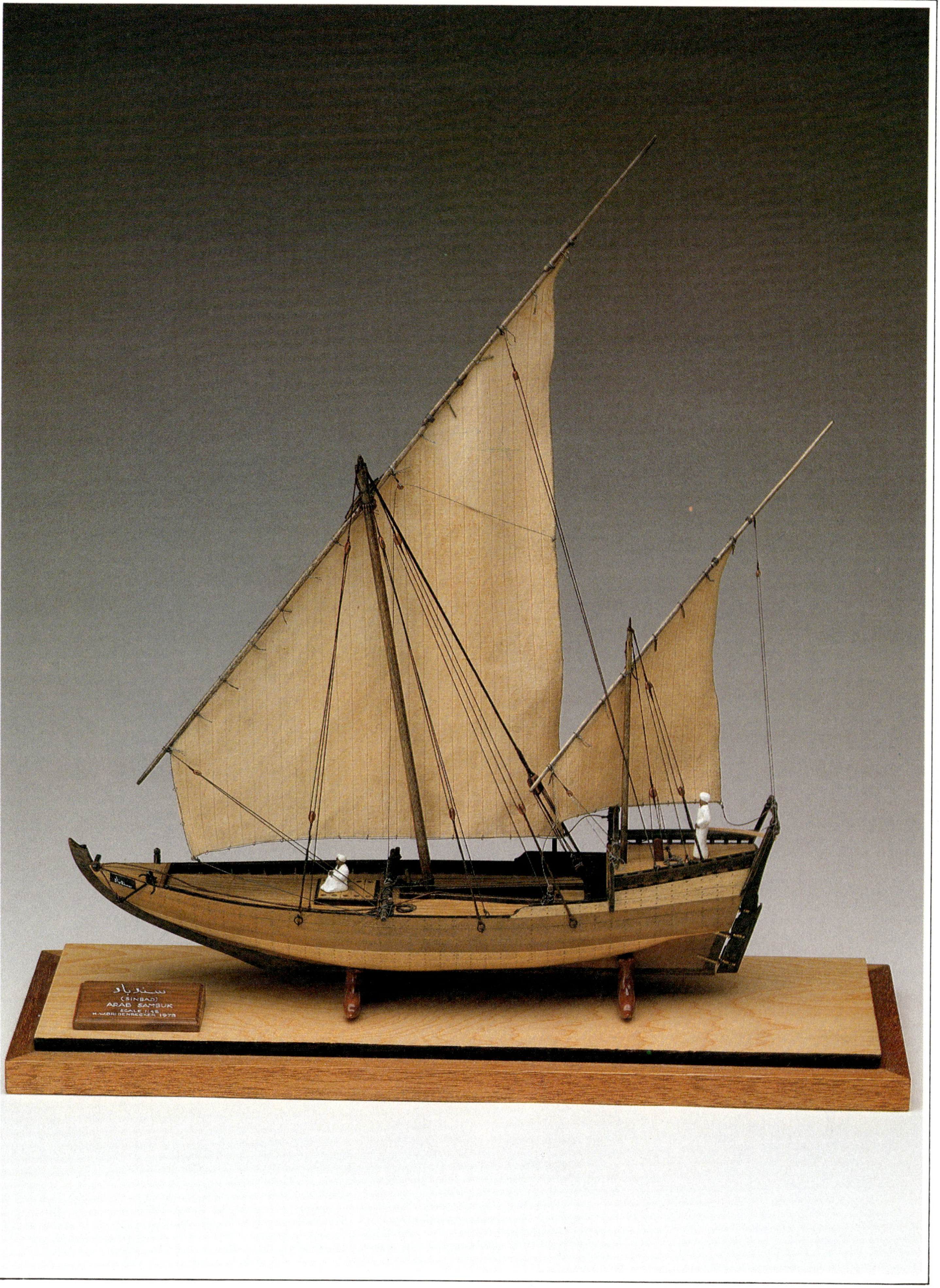

سندباد
(SINBAD)
ARAB SAMBUK
SCALE 1:48
H.W.BRIDENBECKER 1978

A CHINESE WAR JUNK, 19TH CENTURY

This model was of a 19th century Chinese war junk. The plans for the three masted fighting vessel were also made by Vincenzo Lusci. The ship was 100 feet long, 25 feet wide, and carried a crew of over 200 men. It was used by pirates and warlords on the rivers of China and on the China coast.

The construction of junks hasn't changed much since the 13th century. The hull was divided into many compartments by bulkheads made up of thick planks joined together. The system protected the vessel in case of a leak. Leaks happened often enough when the junks ran into reefs in the South China Sea. The Chinese developed the principle of water tight compartments long before the Europeans caught on to the safety feature.

The stern of the junk was richly decorated. The great rudder was perforated with diamond shaped holes for easier steering and it could be hauled up by tackle and windlass in shallow water. The rudder also served as a centerboard. The junk had no keel.

The sails were stiffened by bamboo battens and were furled by lowering and folding at each batten, very much like a venetian blind.

My model was made by fitting planks over several preformed bulkheads. The scale is 1/8" = 1'0". I made the decks of teakwood planks and the hull planks of basswood. The caprails and wales are fine-grained white oak; the boat davits, catheads, blocks, and deadeyes are all Swiss pear. Both *sampans* (ship's boats) were built plank-on-frame over preformed molds of balsa wood. You can see daylight through the planks they are so thin.

The two crew members were originally 1/8' = 1'-0" scale model railroad trainmen, but my wife, Phyllis, converted them to Chinese sailors with a little carving, paint, and the addition of coolie hats.

SIBERIA
VLADIVOSTOK
SEA OF JAPAN
JAPAN
BEIJING (PEKING)
TIANJIN
SEOUL
KOREA
YELLOW SEA
YELLOW RIVER
SHANGHAI
EAST CHINA SEA
PACIFIC OCEAN
YANGTZE RIVER
CHINA
TAIWAN
CANTON
HONG KONG
MANILA
PHILIPPINE ISLANDS
VIETNAM
BORNEO

A Chinese War Junk
Length—100'-0"
Beam—25'-0"
Model Scale—1/8"= 1'-0"

CHINESE SHIPS— MARCO POLO 1292 AD

"We shall commence with a description of the ships employed by the (Chinese) merchants, which are built of fir-timber. They have a single deck ... They are provided with a good helm. They have four masts, with as many sails, and some of them have two masts which can be set up and lowered again, ... Some ships ... have ... to the number of thirteen bulk-heads or divisions in the hold, formed of thick planks let into each other (mortised). The object of these is to guard against accidents which may occasion the vessels to spring a leak, such as striking on a rock or receiving a stroke from a whale, ...

"The ships are all double planked ... These are caulked with oakum both withinside and without, and are fastened with iron nails. They are not coated with pitch, ... but the bottoms are smeared over with ... quick-lime and hemp (mixed with) oil procured from a certain tree ..."

—*The Travels of Marco Polo*

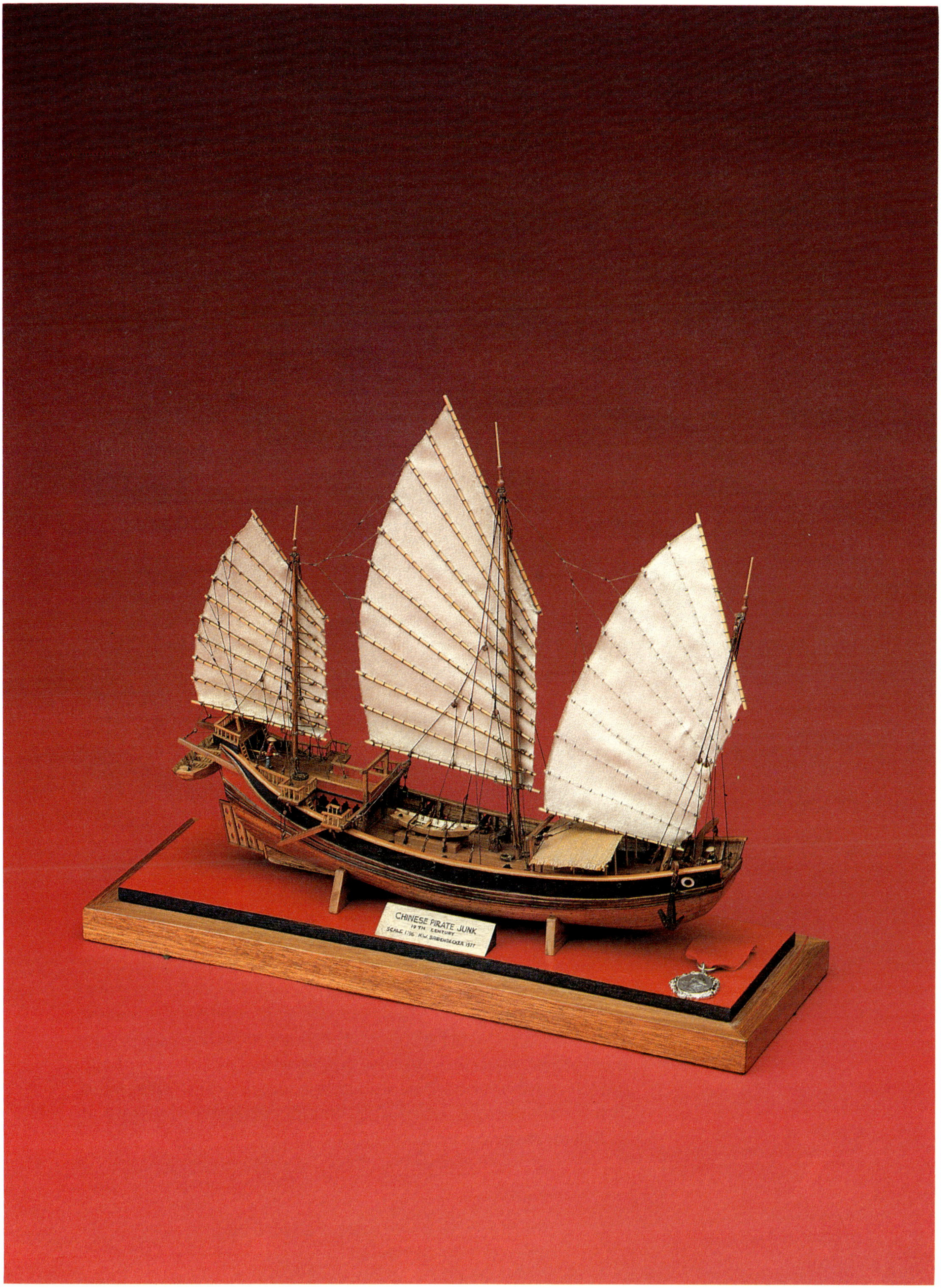
CHINESE PIRATE JUNK
19TH CENTURY
SCALE 1:96

SHIP BUILDING IN COLONIAL AMERICA

No sooner did the early American Colonists touch foot on the shores of the new world than they needed ships.

The Dutch anticipated this need more than the English and were careful to include among their settlers in New Amsterdam some skilled shipwrights.

The English settlements of the eastern seaboard at first had but a handful of men acquainted with the art of ship building, so many of the first small boats built by Englishmen were rather crude and amateurish affairs.

The first ship of any size to be built in English America, as far as we know, was the Virginia, a 30 ton pinnace built in 1607. I selected the Virginia as a modeling project so there will be more about her later.

In 1615–1616 a Dutchman, Adrian Blok, built a *jacht* he called the *Onrust*, of 16 tons. She was a vessel of about 45 feet in length and 11 feet in beam and probably similar in appearance (but less fancy) than the Dutch "Statenjachts" (yachts of state) of the 17th century. Blok explored Long Island Sound and Delaware Bay in her.

By 1630 the North American colonies were well enough established to have the beginnings of a real ship building industry. Shipyards grew up at the mouths of the rivers Merrimac, Mystic, Charles, Connecticut, and Hudson. Seaside towns, honored with a convenient bay and access to the great inland timber resources of the land, also became sites of new shipyards. Among these were Newport, Rhode Island, Ipswich, Boston and Salem in Massachusetts; New London and New Haven in Connecticut; and New York. Though the records are scant, it seems certain that similar boatyards were in action in Virginia, at Baltimore, and on south through the Carolinas.

By 1640 Americans were launching hundreds of small vessels from 25 to 70 tons burthen, and occasionally some larger ships, some of them built for export.
gan in the yard or loft where the builder laid out his ship full scale with a compass, straight edge and plumb line.

By 1700 Colonial ship builders were enjoying a thriving trade. Lord Bellomont, royal governor of New York, declared, "there are more good vessels belonging to the town of Boston than to all of Scotland and Ireland." Ships, together with profitable cargos, made up a lively export trade. By the eve of the American Revolution Boston had become the third port of the British empire and Colonial ship builders had built a full third of all British shipping tonnage in the world.

THE VIRGINIA OF THE SAGADAHOCK

In 1583 Sir Walter Raleigh was out of work even though Queen Elizabeth counted him her favorite courtier. To solve his problem he decided to promote a colony in North America. Since Elizabeth was known as "The Virgin Queen" his colony would be called Virginia. Its main purpose would be to provide a haven for English privateers so they could more easily prey on the Spanish ships to the south.

Two years later, in 1585, a settlement appeared on Roanoke Island. By 1587 the settlement disappeared, but not before it had prepared the way for a more lasting success at Jamestown in May 1607.

Among Raleigh's associates in the Virginia Company were his half brother, Sir Humphrey Gilbert, the Earl of Southhampton, and Sir Ferdinando Gorges. Gilbert had tried in 1583 to set up a colony in America but with less luck than Raleigh on his first try. But once the trials of England with the Spanish Armada in 1588 were over, the Earl of Southhampton revived the colonial action.

The earl sent George Weymouth, in 1605, to explore the Maine coast. Weymouth kidnapped five Indians on his expedition and carried them back to England where three of them stayed with Sir Ferdinando. Inspired, Sir Ferdinando took his turn at sponsoring a colony.

In 1605 a second Virginia Company was set up. The first became known as the "London" or *South Virginia Company*; the second, the "Plymouth" or *North Virginia Company*. King James issued the new patents. The London Company, South Virginia, went on to found Jamestown in 1607 under John Smith.

Gorges picked George Popham and Raleigh Gilbert, Sir Humphrey's son, to lead his band of 120 intrepid settlers for North Virginia. They set out in the spring of 1607 and finally set up their colony on Stage Island at the mouth of the Sagadahock River (Kennebec), in August. There they built the *Virginia* with visions of the riches they would reap from fishing on the Grand Banks.

The *Virginia* of the
Sagadahock
Length—55'-0"±
Beam—14'-0"±
Model Scale 1/8" = 1'-0"

Virginia was launched in October. In December 70 of the original 120 souls in the group had had enough Maine winter and went home to England. George Popham, among others that stayed, died before the winter was done. Finally, in the fall of 1608, all the remaining hands went aboard *Virginia* and sailed home.

Thereafter *Virginia* sailed to and fro between England and successful Jamestown with cargos of goods and tobacco until finally she was wrecked off the Irish coast in 1627.

My model of the pinnace is built to a scale of 1/8" = 1'-0". At this small scale some of the fittings were difficult to build, particularly the functional units such as the rudder hardware and the windlass drum. The model is planked with basswood over a solid hull of alder. The deck planks are holly. The wales are walnut. I used Swiss pear, rosewood, and poplar for deck fixtures and other items.

The U.S. Post Office issued a three cent stamp in 1957 commemorating the *Virginia* which I have framed and mounted in the case with the model.

The model was built from plans drawn by C. M. Langbehn which appeared in the June 1977 issue of the *Nautical Research Journal*.

VIRGINIA 1607
1607 SHIPBUILDING 1957
UNITED STATES POSTAGE

A COLONIAL BARK, 1640 AD

The term "bark" as it was used in Colonial days, is an ambiguous one. Unlike its meaning in the 19th century when the term referred to a specific rig, a colonial bark might be rigged as a sloop, a ketch, a brigantine or even a ship. One gets the impression that a "bark" in the old days was simply a general term for a smallish sort of vessel. In Spanish the general term for vessel is "barca," and in French it is "barque."

Around 1600 Shakespeare used the term in *The Tempest*.
"In few, they hurried us aboard a bark,
Bore us some leagues to sea; where they prepar'd
A rotten carcass of a boat, not rigged, . . ."

Howard Chapelle describes colonial barks as . . . "square-sterned carriers, usually flush-decked" . . . (and a bark) . . . "was a ship builder's name for a hull type."

My model of a Colonial bark was built from drawings made by the late William A. Baker, a naval architect and pre-eminent naval historian. Mr. Baker's reconstruction of a typical 17th century North American trading vessel meets most of Mr. Chapelle's criteria, except she is not "square-sterned." Baker's bark is almost a double-ender, exhibiting many features of Dutch boats of the period.

Baker's Dutch interpretation is logical for 1640, since the early Dutch colonists included more shipwrights in their number than did the English. Such Englishmen who turned to boat building would certainly have learned from the Dutch example.

Chapelle's "square-sterned" vessels, on the other hand, may have been the rule later in the Colonial period.

Baker's bark is a vessel of 29 tons burthen, 46'–0" long between the posts, about 14'–0 in beam, and 6'–0" deep. She carried a hooker rig, two masts with a square sail on each. The foremast is stepped far forward and rakes forward so that the yard hangs out forward of the stem.

The bowsprit carries no head sails but is used exclusively to support the forestay and the tacks of the foresail.

The bark accommodates a crew of eight; four forward, and four aft.

My model is to a scale of 1/4"=1'–0" and is built frame for frame, just as Baker drew her up.

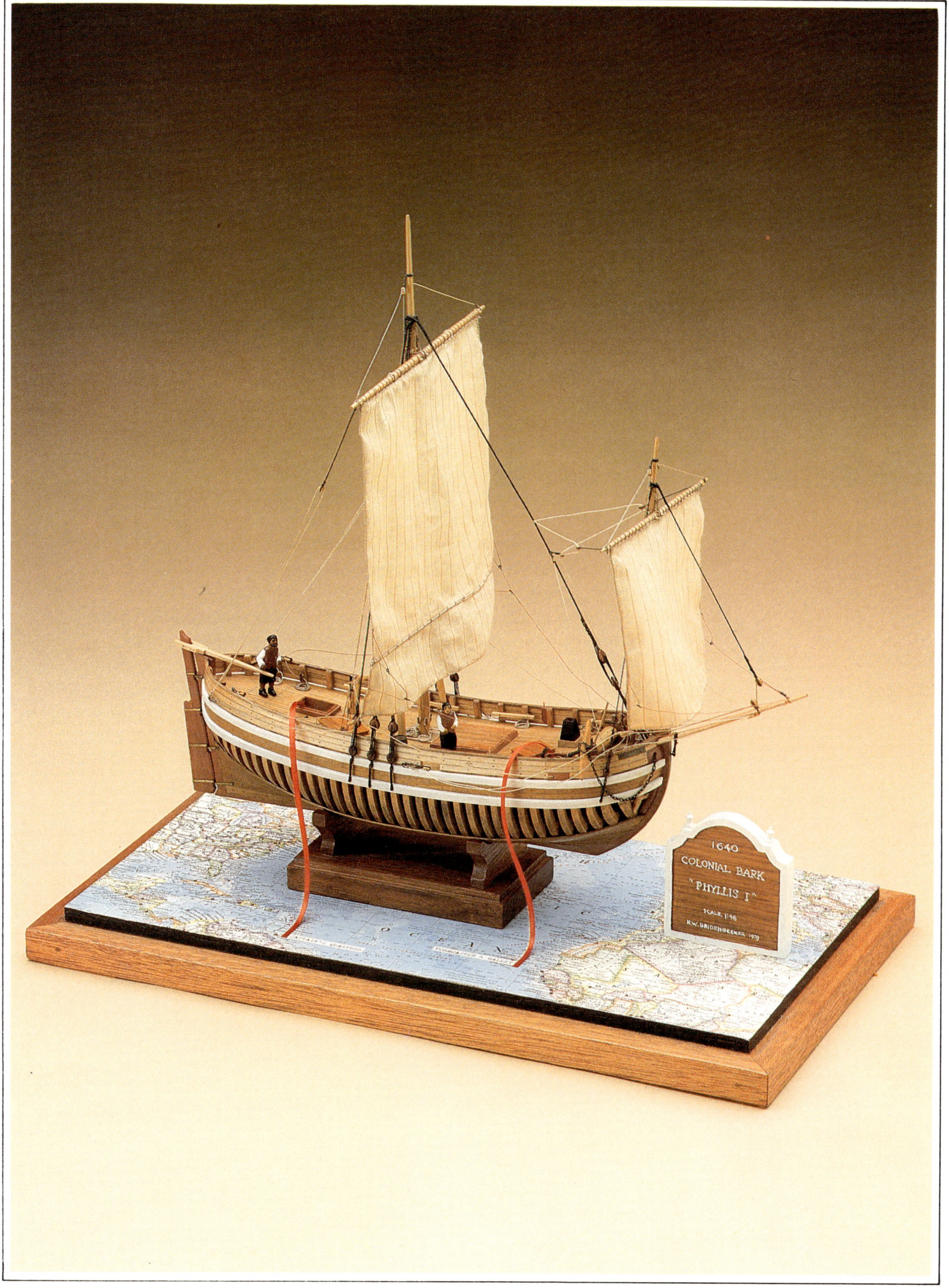
1640
COLONIAL BARK
"PHYLLIS I"

THE HANNAH, A COLONIAL SCHOONER, 1775 AD

Ships classed as "schooners" first appeared in the American registries in 1717. Legend declares that ships of this rig were "invented" in Gloucester, Massachusetts about 1710, but in fact the rig was well known in Europe long before. The Dutch seem to have been the originators.

Still, even if the Gloucestermen didn't invent the schooner, they certainly developed and refined it into a uniquely American type of ship designed and built for fishing on the New England banks.

The small schooners of the colonial period were strictly two masted fore and aft rigged vessels. The larger schooners carried one or more topsails on the foremast and so approached brigantine rigs.

Hannah was one of a flotilla of fishing schooners built and owned by John Glover of Marblehead a bit north of Boston. The Marbleheaders were everything their name implies—hardheaded, tough and virulently independent fisherfolk, acknowledged by even the most independent of New Englanders as a unique breed. They even spoke their own English dialect.

At the outbreak of the American Revolution, Colonel John Glover's regiment of Minutemen, mostly fishermen, were foremost among the patriots because England tried to take away their fishing rights. George Washington approved of Glover's men as he did of Colonel Glover himself. The Marbleheaders, accustomed to taking orders on shipboard, were the only disciplined troops in Washington's army.

Washington leased Glover's *Hannah* for "$1.00 per ton per month" and had her refitted for war at Glover's wharf in Beverly. *Hannah* became the first ship commissioned in the Continental navy. Washington proposed to use her to disrupt British supply lines and capture gun powder for his ill equipped army.

Gun ports were cut in *Hannah*'s sides to accommodate several small 4 pound cannon. The interior was converted from a fish hold into quarters for 35 sailors. And, to give her more speed, topsails were added. *Hannah* became a topsail schooner.

On August 1, 1775 *Hannah* was ready. Thirty-five of Glover's Minuteman sailors, under command of a Captain Broughton, were enlisted as crew, and *Hannah* went to sea in search of prey.

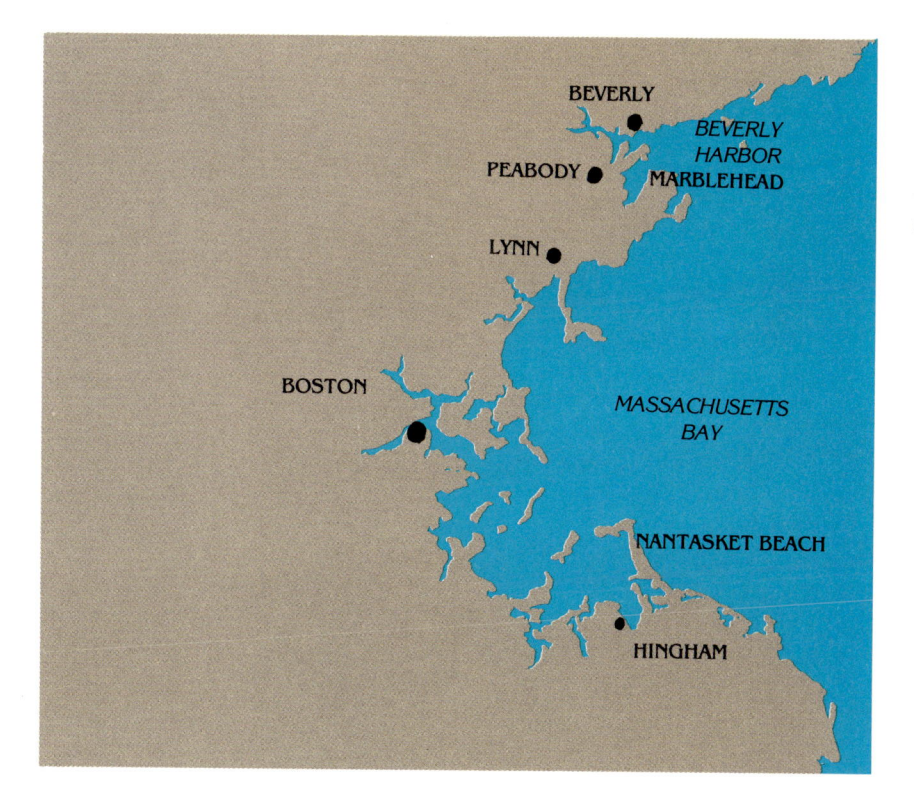

BOSTON AND MASSACHUSETTS BAY HANNAH'S AREA OF OPERATION

A few weeks later she recaptured an American ship—the *Unity*. The crew returned to Boston triumphant expecting prize shares for their trouble. Washington disappointed them declaring that they had not captured a British ship, but an American one, and so were not entitled to prize money. Outraged, the crew mutinied. Washington retaliated with fines and other punishments and ordered a new crew aboard *Hannah*.

Captain Broughton, being a family man, wished to spend evenings with his wife and children and not take unnecessary risks. So his battle tactics were to take *Hannah* to sea during the day, carefully avoid unpleasant encounters with the British, and return to Boston by suppertime. George Washington finally had to explain the program to him.

Hannah set to sea again, this time seriously seeking the British, and unfortunately encountered them in a 16 gun sloop-of-war, the *Nautilus*. This was a bit *too much* British for *Hannah*, so she sailed for shoal water where the sloop dared not go. But the shoals were even too shallow for *Hannah* and she ran aground. The sloop was within range and ready to fire when she too went aground.

59

The *Hannah* of Marblehead
60′-2″ Length
18′-1″ Beam
Depth in Hold 8′-0″
Burthen in Tons 78
Model Scale—1/4″=1′-0″

Hannah's crew, saved by a miracle, took advantage of the situation and shipped their guns ashore where they blazed away at *Nautilus*. But *Nautilus* was out of range and no damage was done.

Finally the tide came in and refloated *Nautilus*. The *Nautilus* sailed away. *Hannah* survived, not to fight, but to fish another day. Washington discharged *Hannah* from military service October 21, 1775, two months and 21 days after her induction. Such was the beginning of America's navy.

My model of *Hannah* is built to a scale of 1/4″=1′-0″ from drawings by Howard Chapelle and Merrit Edson, Jr. I redrew the line drawings to 1/4″ scale and laid out the 34 frames and cant frames required. The model is held together with about 2,800 bamboo dowels, and constructed with: white oak—keel, sternpost, and stem; basswood—hull planks; teak—deck planks; alder—frames, deck beams, and interior structural members; Swiss pear—wales, fashion pieces, cap rails, tiller, and deadeyes, birch—masts, spars and winch; ebony—pumps and gun carriages; boxwood—blocks, compass box, and deck structures. About 1,000 hours spent in building the *Hannah*.

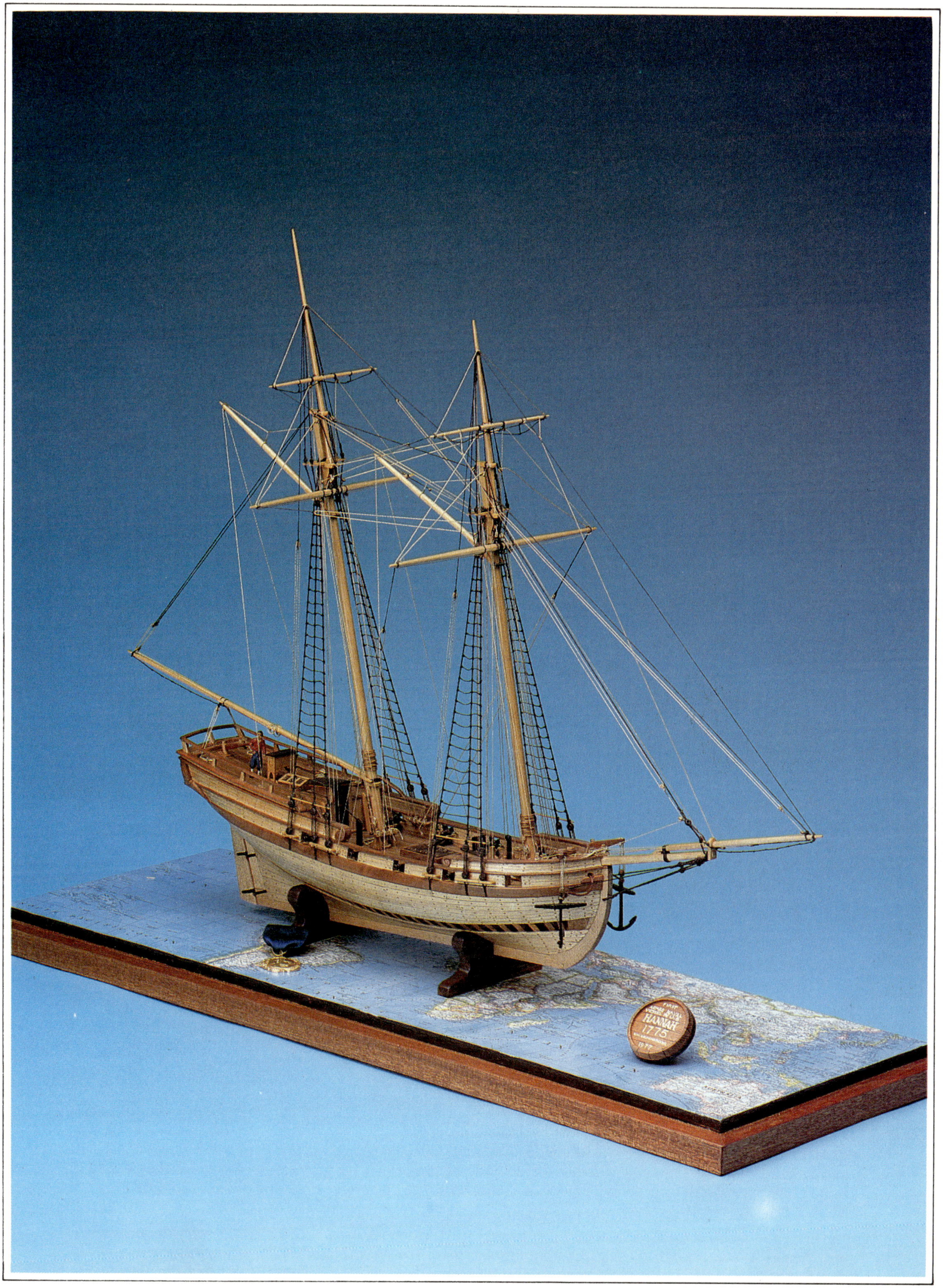
HANNAH
1775

We do not know exactly what *Hannah* was like in all details since no records or drawings of her have survived. It may have been that no drawings of her were ever made. My model is a reconstruction of a typical Marblehead fishing schooner of *Hannah*'s period, the *Sir Edward Hawke*. The plans were drawn by Howard Chapelle and Merrit Edson Jr.

The deck arrangement on my model is one of several such arrangements where the crew sleeps aft under the quarterdeck. The forecastle was used for stowing ship's gear. The crew of later fishing schooners traditionally slept forward. "Back aft" was "officer country." The Marbleheaders, clearly, disliked such class distinctions.

This view of Hannah's stern shows the shape of her underbody in the run. Overall Hannah's lines suggest that she would have been a pretty good sailer in moderate winds, but poor when beating to windward in heavy weather.

A TANCOOK WHALER 1900 AD

Tancook Island, Nova Scotia, lies 30 miles southwest of Halifax. It's a large island with no natural harbor, exposed to the mean, frigid weather of the North Atlantic coast. Its people settled there because of its nearness to the most famous of the world's fishing holes, the Grand Banks.

The fishermen of Tancook needed tough, weatherly boats that could survive heavy seas when moored, unsheltered, offshore, yet light enough to be rowed to the fishing grounds during flat, summer calms.

Tancook's boat builders satisfied the requirements with their "whaler." In spite of her name, the double ended craft with her raking stern post and bald clipper bow, never chased whales. The name derived from the circumstance that for years the Tancook boat builders had earned a good living supplying whaleboats to the New Bedford whaling industry. They knew well how to build whaleboats. So when the time came to build fishing boats for themselves, they adapted their technology to the need and their extraordinary fishing boats became known as Tancook Whalers.

The first of the whalers went to sea about 1865. Thereafter the design was refined and improved until by 1900 it had reached its optimum level of efficiency.

The whalers were carvel planked, schooner rigged, and fitted with a boiler plate center board. They also carried stone ballast.

My model of the whaler is to a scale of 3/8" = 1'–0". It represents a vessel 40' long, 9'–8" in beam, with a draft at the sternpost of 4'–0" with center board up. Howard Chappelle drew the lines for the boat after taking them off an old hulk at Middle River, Nova Scotia, in 1948. I took them from his book *American Small Sailing Craft*, and followed his detailed construction drawings and notes.

I built the model over a carved mold and put it together in the same manner as the original. The keel, stern and sternpost were set up in grooves carved into the mold. Then I bent 50 birch frames into place after soaking the wood stock in ammonia. I planked her up, then removed the hull from the mold and added the ceiling (inside planking) in the forward cabin and cockpit.

I built up the decks, coamings, bulkheads, and added two berths and a stove to make her homey.

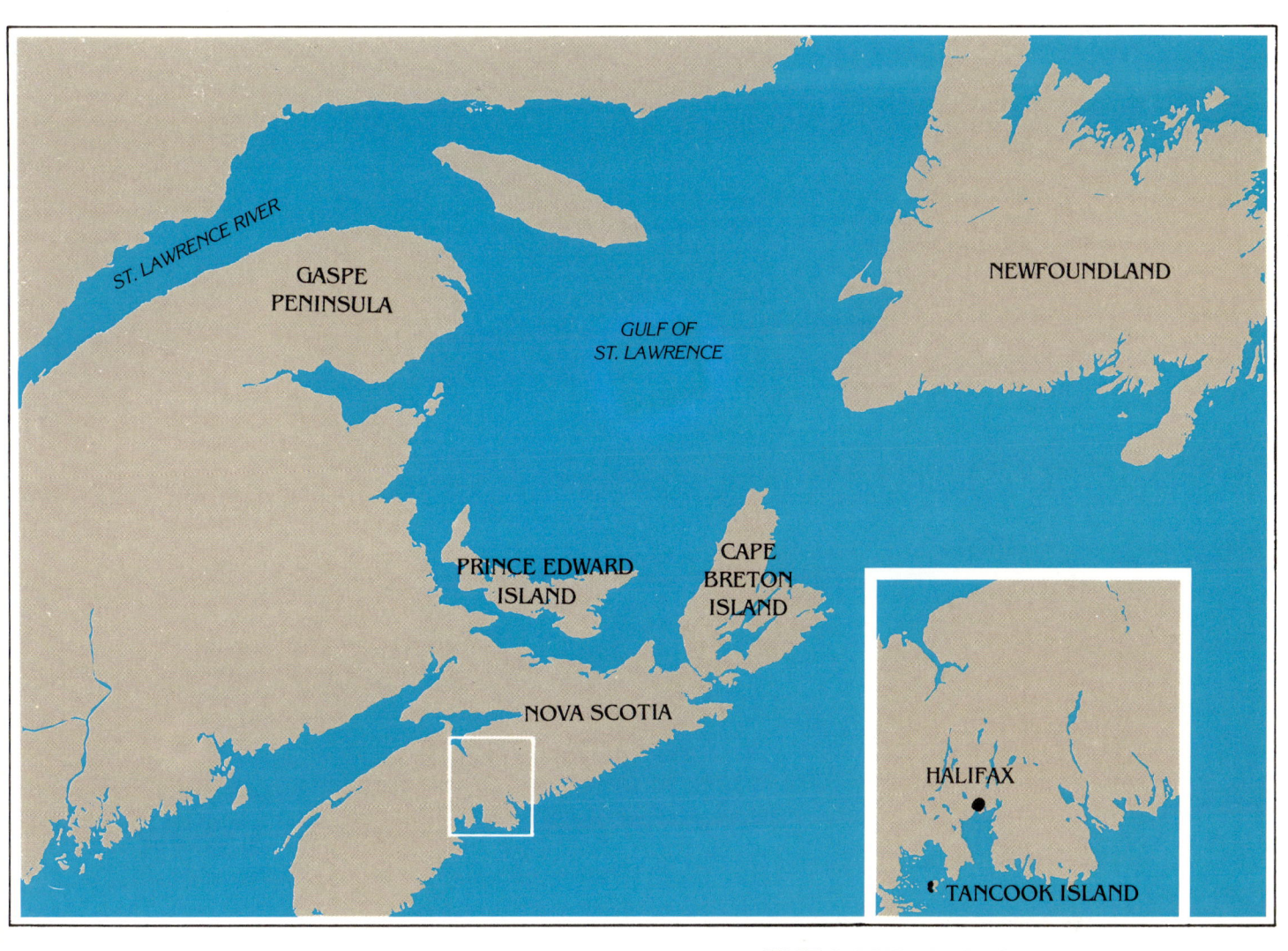

THE LAND AND SEA
AROUND TANCOOK ISLAND

A Tancook Whaler
Length—40'-0"
Beam—9'-8"
Draft—4'-0"(centerboard up)
Model Scale 3/8" =1'0"

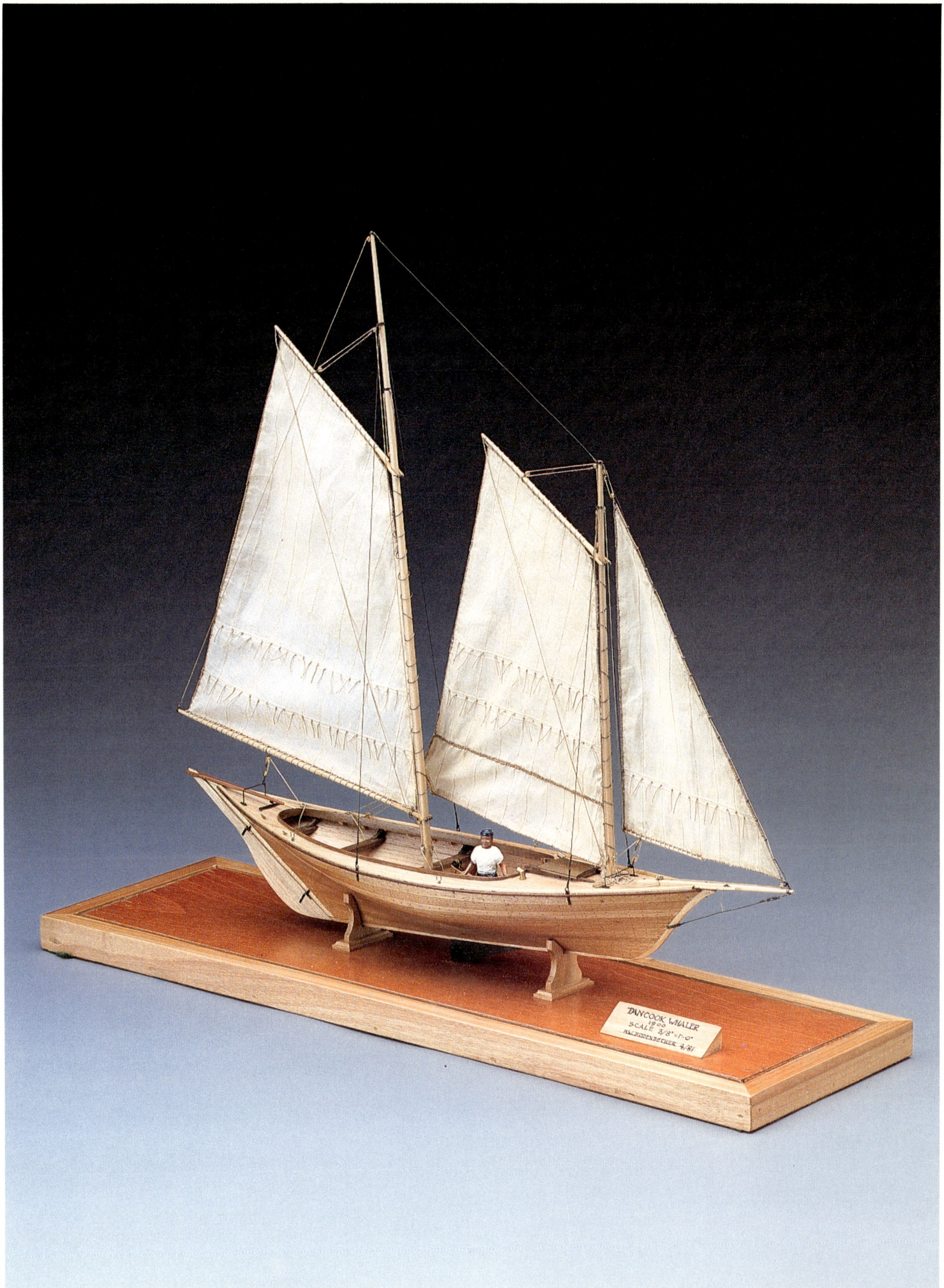
TANCOOK WHALER
1900
SCALE 3/8"=1'-0"

A Tancook whaler's sharp, raked stern was designed to cut and spread out a following sea. This feature allowed the boats to be moored offshore with their sterns pointed seaward, without danger of being pooped.

Captain Joshua Slocum sailed out of Boston Harbor, April 24, 1895, by himself in a 36 foot sloop. Captain Slocum was 51 years old; the sloop was called *Spray*.

Three years and three months later, after a voyage of 46,000 miles under sail alone, *Spray* and Slocum arrived at Newport, Rhode Island. Afterward Slocum wrote a book about his adventures which has since become a classic of the sea—*Sailing Alone Around the World.* The book first appeared in 1898 and has not been out of print since.

Josh Slocum's voyage carried him first across the Atlantic to Gibralter, then back again to the coast of Brazil. He sailed south to the Straits of Magellan, ran the gauntlet into the Pacific, and on to Australia. He crossed the Indian Ocean, rounded the Cape of Good Hope, then headed northwest across the Atlantic for the third time, to home. Josh Slocum's epic voyage inspired a century of adventurous yachtsmen with dreams of single handed wandering.

The original *Spray* was a derelict oyster boat Josh picked up for a song through a friend of his. Slocum rebuilt her plank by plank at a total cost of $553.62 over a period of 13 months. She was 35'-9"long with a beam of 4'-2" and 4'-0" in depth of hold.

I built my model from the drawings in the captain's book. I redrew them up to a scale of 3/8"= 1'-0". Structurally, the model is an exact match of the original.

I fitted out the interior with its bunk, shelves, lockers, a galley stove and other items old Josh had along to keep him company. I made the two cabin trunks removable so one can see the detail below.

The little tender is a "sawed off" Cape Ann dory.

The frames of my *Spray* are alder, the planks poplar, wales walnut, deck planks, dory and cabin trunks willow, and the spars are birch. The dory has birch ribs.

SPRAY, CAPTAIN SLOCUM'S SLOOP 1895

The *Spray*
Length—35'-9"
Beam— 4'-2"
Depth of Hold-4'-0"
Model Scale—3/8" = 1'-0'

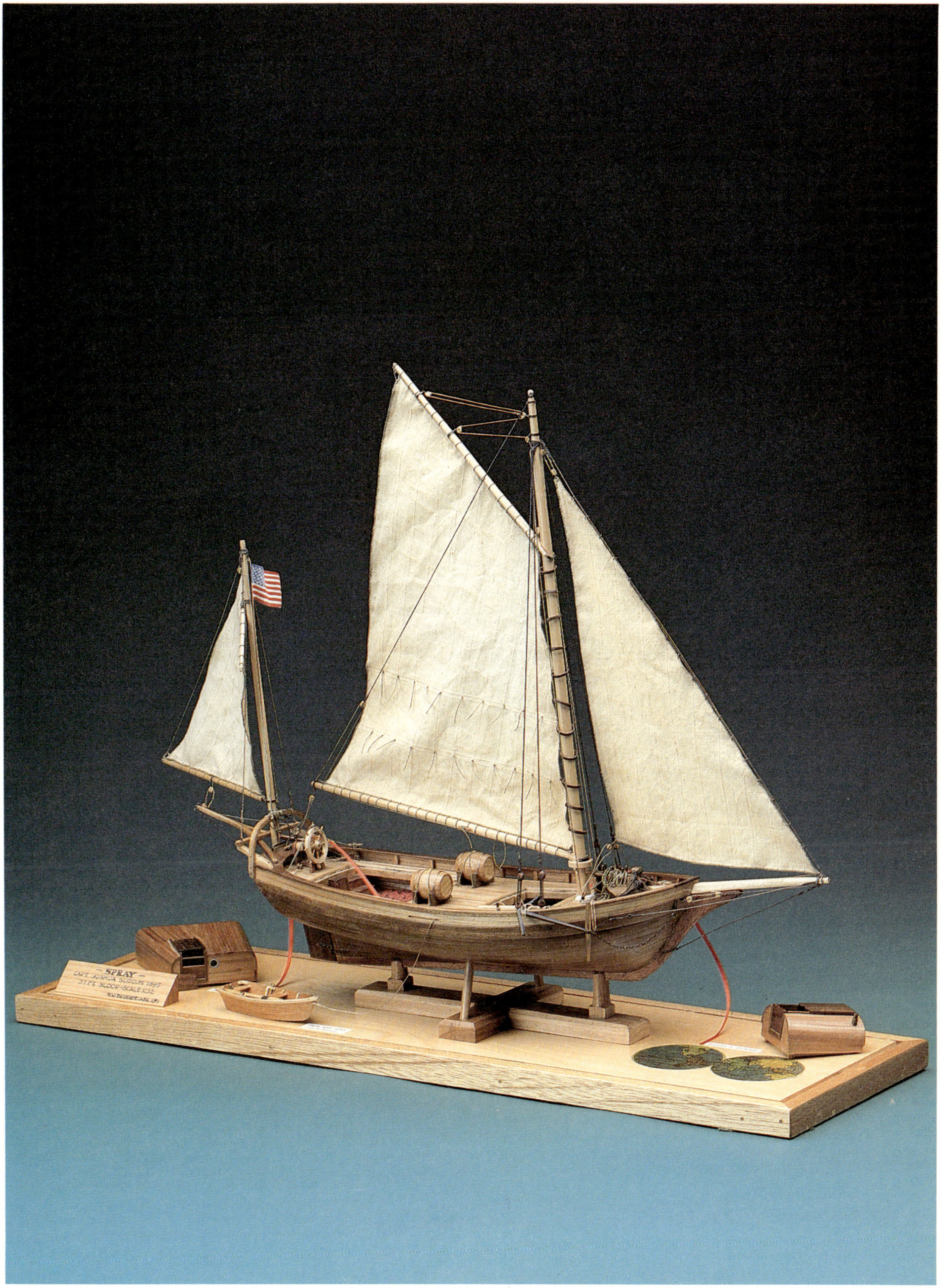
SPRAY

Captain Slocum rerigged *Spray* as a yawl after his first trans-Atlantic passage. The little mizzen mast stepped at the taffrail provided him a self-steering mechanism, similar in principle, to that of modern yachts. The sheet of the mizzen sail bent to the wheel served to keep the boat on a steady course by pressing down the helm as soon as the vessel fell away to leeward.

Captain Slocum stowed his stores forward. The two kegs on deck held his supply of fresh drinking water.

73

A U.S. Navy Anchor Hoy
Length—56'-9"
Beam—20'-0"
Model Scale 3/16" = 1'-0"

A U.S. NAVY ANCHOR HOY, 1820

Anchor hoys once plied the harbors of the world much as tugboats do today. Their purpose in life was to assist larger ships in coming to anchor in congested waterways.

A properly anchored ship requires that the anchor be dug into the sea bottom some yards away from the ship itself so that the cable will drape up to the ship in a long, flat curve. If a ship has maneuvering room, she can drop her hook and drift off to a proper cable distance. Lacking such room, however, she'd call for a hoy. The hoy would come alongside, ship her anchor, then carry it out a distance and drop it for her.

The hoys were designed and equipped specifically to handle these huge anchors, but they also carried provisions and gear from shore to ship and performed all sorts of service duties.

My model of a hoy is of a U.S. Navy version of about 1820. The plans for her were drawn by Francis Grice, a ship designer of the period, whose original drawings are preserved in the Office of Naval Records and Library in Washington D.C. I took the data and plans from V.R. Grimwood's book *American Sailing Vessels*.

The boat is 56'–9" long with a beam of 20'–0". The shrouds of the mast were set low to support the heavy anchor handling gear. There are two capstans. The one forward hauls in the cable. It goes unmanned but is geared to the after capstan in a system designed to conserve manpower. Men turn the after capstan which operates the forward one. The bowsprit is offset to accommodate the anchor cat occupying the center.

My model is to a scale of 3/16"=1'–0". The ribs and planking are made of poplar, the deck of tupelo woods, and the masts and spars of birch. I used box for some the small fittings.

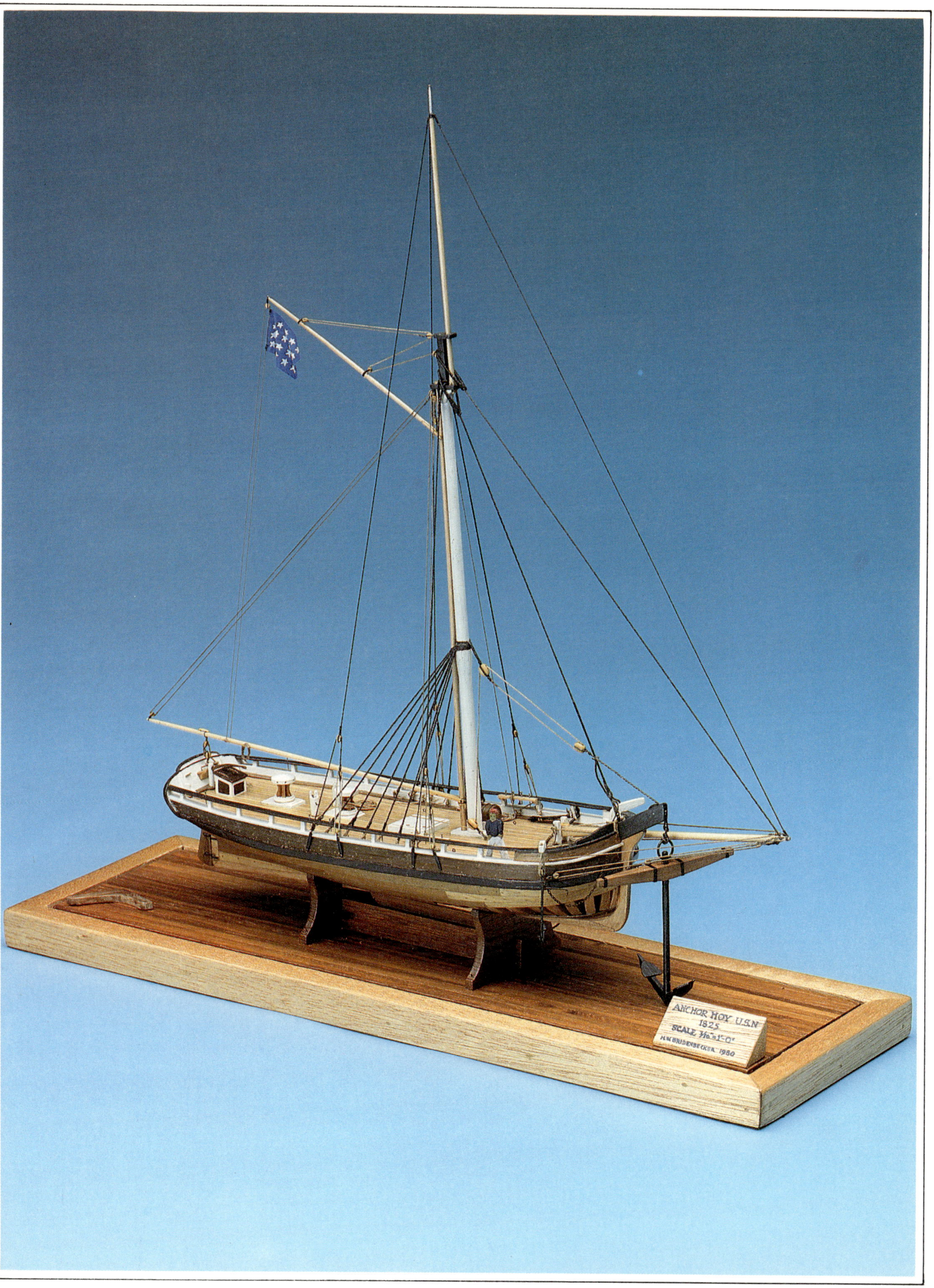
ANCHOR HOY U.S.N
1825
SCALE 1/16"=1'-0"
H.W. BRIDENBECKER 1980

The hauling part of the anchor handling tackle led below decks to an unmanned forward capstan geared to a second capstan aft. The mast shrouds are rigged to support the weight of the large anchors the hoy hove about.

The *Fanny M* of 1886 was known to her contemporaries as a "Piscataqua River Gundalow," a mouthful of name for a strange looking vessel. Presumably the name "gundalow" was adapted from the Italian *gondola* combined with a reference to its ability to negotiate *low* bridges.

The gundalow was a flat-bottomed, lateen rigged craft with a large leeboard on the port side. It was a low cost boat, designed to carry deck loads, particularly loads of lumber, on rivers with many low bridges. As the gundalow reached a low bridge, she dipped her long lateen yard and passed comfortably along.

The Piscataquis River (from which "Piscataqua" derives) in Maine was just such a river. Flowing eastward from its source in the Longfellow Mountains of central Maine, the Piscataquis connected the lumber towns along its bank—Guilford, Dover-Foxcroft, Derby, Medford, and others—with the outside world. The waters of Piscataquis join those of the Penobscot running south through Bangor to Penobscot Bay and the great Atlantic.

One of the most important of Maine's economic resources is her vast stands of timber. In the 1880s this timber was the life blood of the ship builders of the New England coast. The *Fanny M* was built mainly to carry timber to the shipyards and so played a double role in our maritime past.

The *Fanny M* was built by Captain Adams of Adams Point, Massachusetts in 1886. Mr. D.F. Taylor of Massachusetts used the original builder's model, as well as the abandoned wreck of the hull, to make measured drawings of the lines and details of this vessel. The barge was 68'–10" long and 19'–2" wide. The mast was 19'–2" above the deck and supported a lateen yard 68'–10" long.

FANNY M
A PISCATAQUA
RIVER GUNDALOW,
1886

The *Fanny M*
A Piscataqua River Gundalow
Length—68'-10"
Beam—19'-2"
Model Scale 1/4" = 1'-0"

My model is to a scale of 1/4" =1'-0". The hull is planked with 16 planks to a side over 33 frames. It has a large, four-windowed deck house with a sliding hatch cover all of which may be removed to expose a galley stove, two bunks, a round table and two chairs. A port leeboard 5' wide and 15' long, and reinforced with "iron" straps is attached to the side of the hull. A scratchbuilt ship's wheel 9/16" in diameter, made of Swiss pear with turned brass spokes, is mounted on a shafted drum of alder supported by two brass-bound boxwood "A" frames bolted to the deck. The "iron" tiller is controlled by ropes passing through brass-sheaved boxwood blocks to a wheel drum.

The "asphalted" deck made of fine grit "wet-or-dry" sand paper between the mast and the fore side of the deckhouse is loaded with a cargo of teak, birch, mahogany and pine planks, four hogsheads of molasses, ten boxes of various mechandise, and about four and one-half cubic yards of "coal" made from crushed basalt.

Portable deck rails of mahogany planks provide a retaining space for the deck loads. The huge lateen yard is secured to the stubby mast by a heavy chain halliard. The tack tackle at the lower end of the yard consists of two double-sheaved blocks tied into metal bands at the foot of the yard, and to the base of the mast. The lateen sail is fastened with stops to the 68' yard. The continuous brail reef rope passed through cringles formed in the bolt rope of the sail, and through ten single blocks on the yard where it is finally belayed to a cleat on the forward side of the yard near the foot. The main sheet tackle is fastened to a traveler ring on the iron horse crossing over the deckhouse roof. The topping lift is belayed to a cleat at the stern rail.

Wood used in the construction:
    Alder frames and hull planking.
    Dark poplar keel, stem and stern piece, deck rails, hatch coamings.
    Willow deck planks and hatch covers.
    Bamboo dowel fastenings.

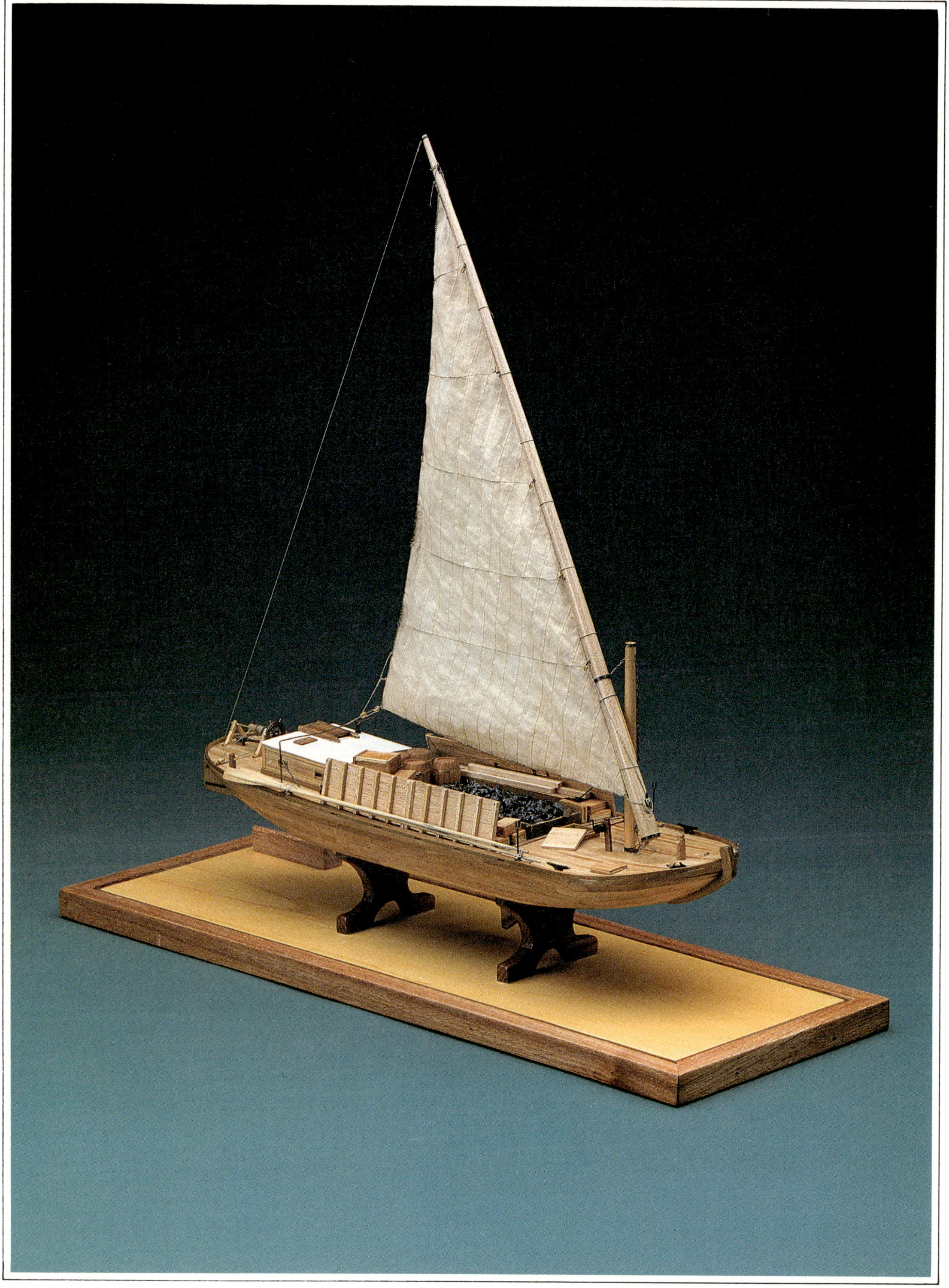

The gundalow navigated under sail offshore with her lee board down. She carried a lee board on her port side only. When the "lee" board was in fact to windward an iron bar kept it from being carried away.
The washboards were set up only when a deck cargo had to be protected from the seas. Otherwise they were taken down and stowed on deck.

The unpretentious gundalow I have just described is, to me, a fitting conclusion to a discussion of my ship modeling projects to date. She summarizes my feelings about the subject. I am interested in the life and times of the ordinary sailors and the ship builders of the past, whose labor, craftsmanship and love of the sea make up the real panorama of maritime history, if not the history of men in general.

The gundalow, simple, tough, contributing as she did to the building of other ships and her New England home of the 1880s, seems to reflect the spirit of Henry Wadsworth Longfellow's poem, *The Building of the Ship*. The poem also says a lot about why ship modelers, like me, do what we do.

The Building of the Ship
by Henry Wadsworth Longfellow

"Build me straight, O worthy Master!
    Staunch and strong, a goodly vessel
That shall laugh at all disaster,
    And with wave and whirlwind wrestle!"

The merchant's word
Delighted the Master heard;
For his heart was in his work, and the heart
Giveth grace unto every Art.
A quiet smile played round his lips,
As the eddies and dimples of the tide
Play round the bows of ships,
That steadily at anchor ride.
And with a voice that was full of glee,
He answered, "Erelong we will launch
A vessel as goodly, and strong, and staunch,
As ever weathered a wintry sea!"
And first with nicest skill and art,
Perfect and finished in every part,
A little model the Master wrought,
Which should be to the larger plan
What the child is to the man,
Its counterpart in miniature;
That with a hand more swift and sure
The greater labor might be brought
To answer to his inward thought.
And as he labored, his mind ran o'er
The various ships that were built of yore,
And above them all, and strangest of all
Towered the Great Harry, crank and tall,
Whose picture was hanging on the wall,
With bows and stern raised high in air,
And balconies hanging here and there,
And signal lanterns and flags afloat,
And eight round towers, like those that frown
From some old castle, looking down
Upon the drawbridge and the moat.
And he said with a smile, "Our ship, I wis,
Shall be of another form than this!"
It was of another form, indeed;
Built for freight, and yet for speed,
A beautiful and gallant craft;

Broad in the beam, that the stress of the blast,
Pressing down upon sail and mast,
Might not the sharp bows overwhelm;
Broad in the beam but sloping aft
With graceful curve and slow degrees,
That she might be docile to the helm,
And that the currents of parted seas,
Closing behind, with mighty force,
Might aid and not impede her course

In the ship-yard stood the Master,
With the model of the vessel,
That should laugh at all disaster,
And with wave and whirlwind wrestle!

Covering many a rood of ground,
Lay the timber piled around;
Timber of chestnut, and elm, and oak,
And scattered here and there, with these,
The knarred and crooked cedar knees;
Brought from regions far away,
From Pascagoula's sunny bay,
And the banks of the roaring Roanoke!
Ah! what a wondrous thing it is
To note how many wheels of toil
One thought, one word, can set in motion!
There's not a ship that sails the ocean,
But every climate, every soil,
Must bring its tribute, great or small,
And help to build the golden wall!

The sun was rising o'er the sea,
And long the lever shadows lay,
As if they, too, the beams would be
Of some great, airy argosy,
Framed and launched in a single day.
That silent architect, the sun,
Had hewn and laid them every one,
Ere the work of man was yet begun.
Beside the Master, when he spoke,
A youth, against an anchor leaning,
Listened, to catch his slightest meaning.

Only the long waves, as they broke
In ripples on the pebbly beach,
Interrupted the old man's speech.
Beautiful they were, in sooth,
The old man and the fiery youth!
The old man, in whose busy brain
Many a ship that sailed the main
Was modelled o'er and o'er again;—
The fiery youth, who was to be
The heir of his dexterity,
The heir of his house, and his daughter's hand,
When he had built and launched from land
What the elder head had planned.

"Thus," said he, "will we build this ship!
Lay square the blocks upon the slip,
And follow well this plan of mine.
Choose the timbers with greatest care;
Of all that is unsound beware;
For only what is sound and strong
To this vessel shall belong.
Cedar of Maine and Georgia pine
Here together shall combine.
A goodly frame, and a goodly fame,
And the UNION be her name!
For the day that gives her to the sea
Shall give my daughter unto thee!"

The Master's word
Enraptured the young man heard;
And as he turned his face aside,
With a look of joy and a thrill of pride
Standing before
Her father's door
He saw the form of his promised bride.
The sun shone on her golden hair,
And her cheek was glowing fresh and fair,
With the breath of morn and the soft sea air.
Like a beauteous barge was she,
Still at rest on the sandy beach,
Just beyond the billow's reach;
Be he

Was the restless, seething, stormy sea!
Ah, how skilful grows the hand
That obeyeth Love's command!
It is the heart, and not the brain,
That to the highest doth attain,
And he who followeth Love's behest
Far excelleth all the rest!

Thus with the rising of the sun
Was the noble task begun,
And soon throughout the ship-yard's bounds
Were heard the intermingled sounds
Of axes and of mallets, plied
With vigorous arms on every side;
Plied so deftly and so well,
That, ere the shadows of evening fell,
The keel of oak for a noble ship,
Scarfed and bolted, straight and strong,
Was lying ready, and stretched along
The blocks, well placed upon the slip.
Happy, thrice happy, every one
Who sees his labor well begun,
And not perplexed and multiplied,
By idly waiting for time and tide!

And when the hot, long day was o'er,
The young man at the Master's door
Sat with the maiden calm and still,
And within the porch, a little more
Removed beyond the evening chill,
As he lies alone and asleep on the turf.
And the trembling maiden held her breath
At the tales of that awful, pitiless sea,
With all its terror and mystery,
The dim, dark sea, so like unto Death,
That divides and yet united mankind!
And whenver the old man paused, a gleam
From the bowl of his pipe would awhile illume
The silent group in the twilight gloom,
And thoughtful faces, as in a dream;
And for a moment one might mark
What had been hidden by the dark,

That the head of the maiden lay at rest,
Tenderly, on the young man's breast!

Day by day the vessel grew,
With timbers fashioned strong and true,
Stemson and keelson and sternson-knee,
Till, framed with perfect symmetry,
A skeleton ship rose up to view!
And around the bows and along the side
The heavy hammers and mallets plied,
Till after many a week, at length,
Wonderful for form and strength,
Sublime in its enormous bulk
Loomed aloft the shadowy hulk!
And around it columns of smoke upwreathing,
Rose from the boiling, bubbling, seething
Caldron, that glowed,
And overflowed
With the black tar, heated for the sheathing.
And amid the clamors
Of clattering hammers,
He who listened heard now and then
The song of the Master and his men:—

"Build me straight, O worthy Master,
   Stanch and strong, a goodly vessel,
That shall laugh at all disaster,
   And with wave and whirlwind wrestle!"

With oaken brace and copper band,
Lay the rudder on the sand,
That, like a thought, should have control
Over the movement of the whole;
And near it the anchor, whose giant hand
Would reach down and grapple with the land,
And immovable and fast
Hold the great ship against the bellowing blast!
And at the bows an image stood,
By the cunning artist carved in wood,
With robes of white, that far behind
Seemed to be fluttering in the wind.
It was not shaped in a classic mould,

Not like a Nymph or Goddess of old,
Or Naiad rising from the water,
But modelled from the Master's daughter!
On many a dreary and misty night,
'T will be seen by the rays of the signal light,
Speeding along through the rain and the dark,
Like a ghost in its snow-white sark,
The pilot of some phantom bark,
Guiding the vessel, in its flight,
By a path none other knows aright!

Behold, at last,
Each tall and tapering mast
Is swung into its place;
Shrouds and stays
Holding it firm and fast!

Long ago,
In the deer-haunted forests of Maine,
When upon mountain and plain
Lay the snow,
They fell,—those lordly pines!
Those grand, majestic pines!
'Mid shouts and cheers
The jaded steers,
Panting beneath the goad,
Dragged down the weary, winding road
Those captive kings so straight and tall,
To be shorn of their streaming hair,
And naked and bare,
To feel the stress and the strain
Of the wind and the reeling main,
Whose roar
Would remind them forevermore
Of their native forests they should not see again.

And everywhere
The slender, graceful spars
Poise aloft in the air,
And at the mast-head,
White, blue, and red,
A flag unrolls the stripes and stars.

83

Ah! when the wanderer, lonely, friendless,
In foreign harbors shall behold
That flag unrolled,
'T will be as a friendly hand
Stretched out from his native land,
Filling his heart with memories sweet and endless!

All is finished! and at length
Has come the bridal day
of beauty and of strength
To-day the vessel shall be launched!
With fleecy clouds the sky is blanched,
And o'er the bay,
Slowly, in all his splendors dight,
The great sun rises to behold the sight.
The oceans old,
Centuries old,
Strong as youth, and as uncontrolled,
Paces restless to and fro,
Up and down the sands of gold.
His beating heart is not at rest;
And far and wide,
With ceaseless flow,
His beard of snow
Heaves with the heaving of his breast.
He waits impatient for his bride.
There she stands,
With her foot upon the sands,
Decked with flags and streamers gay,
In honor of her marriage day,
Her snow-white signals fluttering, blending,
Round her like a veil descending,
Ready to be
The bride of the gray old sea.

On the deck another bride
Is standing by her lover's side.
Shadows from the flags and shrouds,
Like the shadows cast by clouds,
Broken by many a sudden fleck,
Fall around them on the deck.

The prayer is said,
The service read.
The joyous bridegroom bows his head;
And in tears the good old Master
Shakes the brown hand of his son,
Kisses his daughter's glowing cheek
In silence, for he cannot speak,
And ever faster
Down his own the tears begin to run.
The worthy pastor—
The shepherd of that wandering flock,
That has the ocean for its wold,
That has the vessel for its fold,
Leaping ever from rock to rock—
Spake, with accents mild and clear,
Words of warning, words of cheer,
But tedious to the bridegrooms's ear.
He knew the chart
Of the sailor's heart,
All its pleasures and its griefs,
All its shallows and rocky reefs,
All those secret currents, that flow
With such resistless undertow,
And lift and drift, with terrible force,
The will from its moorings and its course.
Therefore he spake, and thus said he:—
"Like unto ship far off at sea,
Outward or homeward bound, are we.
Before, behind, and all around,
Floats and swings the horizon's bound,
Seems at its distant rim to rise
And climb the crystal wall of the skies,
And then again to turn and sink
As if we could slide from its outer brink.
Ah! it is not the sea,
It is not the sea that sinks and shelves,
But ourselves
That rock and rise
With endless and uneasy motion,
Now touching the very skies,
Now sinking into the depths of ocean.
Ah! if our souls but poise and swing

84

Like the compass in its brazen ring,
Ever level and ever true
To the toil and the task we have to do,
We shall sail securely, and safely reach
The Fortunate Isles, on whose shining beach
The sights we see, and the sounds we hear,
Will be those of joy and not of fear!"
Then the Master,
With a gesture of command,
Waved his hand;
And at the word,
Loud and sudden there was heard,
All around them and below,
The sound of hammers, blow on blow,
Knocking away the shores and spurs.
And see! she stirs!
She starts,—she moves,—she seems to feel
The thrill of life along her keel,
And, spurning with her foot the ground,
With one exulting, joyous bound,
She leaps into the ocean's arms!

And lo! from the assembled crowd
There rose a shout, prolonged and loud,
That to the ocean seemed to say,
"Take her, O bridegroom, old and gray,
Take her to thy protecting arms,
With all her youth and all her charms!"

How beautiful she is! How fair
She lies within those arms, that press
Her form with many a soft caress
Of tenderness and watchful care!
Sail forth into the sea, O ship!
Through wind and wave, right onward steer!
The moistened eye, the trembling lip,
Are not the signs of doubt or fear.

Sail forth into the sea of life,
O gentle, loving, trusting wife,
And safe from all diversity
Upon the bosom of that sea

Thy comings and thy goings be!
For gentleness and love and trust
Prevail o'er angry wave and gust;
And in the wreck of noble lives
Something immortal still survives!

Thou, too, sail on, O Ship of State!
Sail on, O Union, strong and great!
Humanity with all its fears,
With all the hopes of future years,
Is hanging breathless on they fate!
We know what Master laid thy keel,
What Workmen wrought thy ribs of steel,
Who made each mast, and sail, and rope,
What anvils rang, what hammers beat,
In what a forge and what a heat
Were shaped the anchors of thy hope!
Fear not each sudden sound and shock,
'T is of the wave and not the rock;
'T is but the flapping of the sail,
And not a rent made by the gale!
In spite of rock and tempest's roar,
In spite of false lights on the shore,
Sail on, nor fear to breast the sea!
Our hearts, our hopes, are all with thee,
Our hearts, our hopes, our prayers, our tears,
Our faith triumphant o'er our fears,
Are all with thee,—are all with thee!

PART II: TIPS FOR THE MODELER

The discussion that follows here is a collection of little tricks and methods I have worked out over the years. It is not intended as a comprehensive treatise on the shipmodeler's craft. The techniques described are more or less a random selection of procedures covering some of the more puzzling and not so puzzling problems I have encountered in my building.

A craftsman contemplating a ship modeling project, I think, will get the idea that there is no single, fixed solution to any of the construction problems ahead of him. A hint here and there from an experienced model shipwright might be useful, but when all is said, one's own ingenuity and imagination must be the final authority.

The very fact that ship modeling requires one to be his own engineer, tool maker, draftsman and materials expert is part of the fun.

FRAME CONSTRUCTION

The distinctive feature of most of my models is that they mimic full-scale ship building practice. Each of the timbers that would occur in the real ship, occur in the model.

Among the most important and perhaps most challenging timbers to make are the frames or ribs of the vessel to which the planks are fastened.

A person looking at a set of ship's plans for the first time will see a set of lines representing the shape of the hull in three views: a side view (sheer plan), one half of a bottom view (half-breadth plan), and a view showing the ship from both ends in one drawing called a "body plan." The body plan shows the shape of transverse sections of the ship at various "stations" along the length of the ship. The stations show up on the sheer and half-breadth plans as lines running perpendicular to the keel, and marked with station numbers or letters.

WATERLINES SHOW UP IN THE *HALF BREADTH* PLAN. THEY SHOW THE SHIP AS IF SLICED HORIZONTALLY THROUGH ITS LENGTH

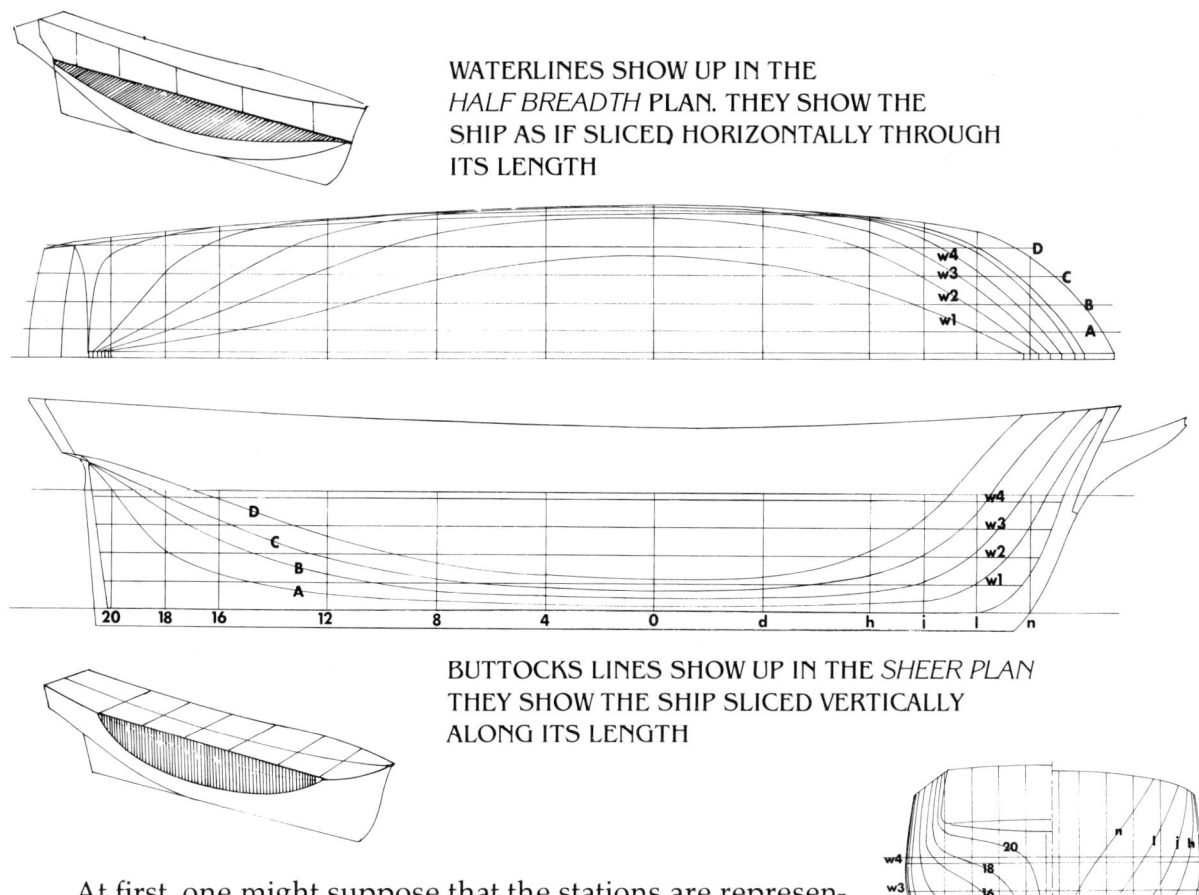

BUTTOCKS LINES SHOW UP IN THE *SHEER PLAN* THEY SHOW THE SHIP SLICED VERTICALLY ALONG ITS LENGTH

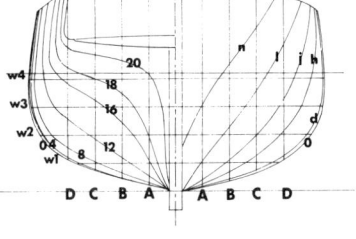

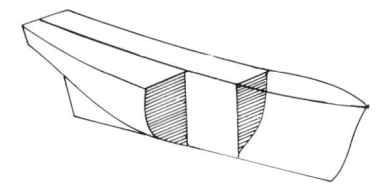

BODY SECTIONS SHOW UP IN THE *BODY PLAN* THEY SHOW THE SHIP SLICED VERTICALLY ATHWARTSHIP

At first, one might suppose that the stations are representations of the frames themselves. Not so. A ship has many more frame timbers than are shown in the lines drawings. Yet the shape of each frame must be interpolated from the architect's lines. This requires some precision drafting.

1. The first step in developing the shape of each frame in the hull, is to plot their positions on the sheer and half-breadth plans. To do this one needs the distance center-to-center of the frames which, among ship builders, is known as "room and space," room being the thickness of the frames; space the air between them. Frequently the "room" in a ship's hull is greater than the space, particularly in warships. The widest station of the hull is the midship section, often designated as 0 on the plans. The stations forward of it are marked a, b, c, etc; those aft 1,2,3... The midship section represents the centerline of the first frame of our concern, from which the positions of all others are measured fore and aft. One represents the forward and after sides of each frame in the sheer and half-breadth plans with lines perpendicular to the keel (parallel with the station lines).

87

FRAME CONSTRUCTION

A TYPICAL FRAME LAYOUT

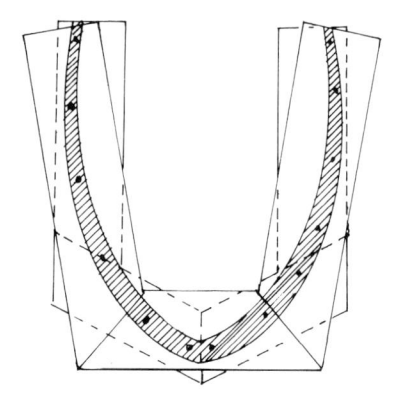

EACH FRAME IS BUILT UP OF TWO LAYERS OF TIMBER AND UP TO SEVEN PIECES JOINTED AND DOWELED TOGETHER

2. The next step is to note that the lines representing the frames in the sheer and half-breadth plans intersect curved lines which represent the hull as if sliced longitudinally. The half-breadth plan shows a series of curves representing horizontal slices taken at regular heights up from the keel. These heights show up in the sheer plan as parallel lines running fore and aft. These are called the "waterlines." The sheer plan shows a set of curves representing slices through the hull in the vertical plane. These lines, called "buttocks," show up in the half-breadth plan as parallel lines at regular distances out from the keel. If one plots the distances "up" and "out" indicated by these lines at each station along the length of the hull, he will obtain a point plot of the sections shown in the body plan.

3. Similarly, the shape of each frame in the ship is a matter of measuring the "ups" and the "outs" for each frame position drawn on the sheer and the half-breadth plans, and plotting these points on the body plan. Then the shape of the frame can be drawn between the points conforming with the curves of the architect's closest body sections. These point plots can be accomplished using draftsman's projection techniques.

4. I plot and draw each frame on a separate piece of tracing paper. The plot, of course, yields only one half of the whole frame, so I fold the tracing paper in half along the centerline and trace off the other half giving me a pattern for the whole frame.

5. The frames toward the bow and stern require bevels to conform with the sides of the ship. So one makes a pattern for both the forward and after edges of the frame.

6. The next step is to draw the inside edges of the frames. One starts again with the midship frame, then uses it as a master pattern for the rest. The idea is to draw the inside of the frames so that the ceiling (inside) planks will lay as fair as the outer planking when the frames are set up.

7. Each frame, in many ships, is a composite affair made up of 7 or more separate pieces of timber, joined so that the grain of the wood runs more or less parallel with the "U" shape of the frame. One commences the construction of a frame by building up a composite "blank" for it, with stock half the thickness of the

FRAME CONSTRUCTION

whole frame (a frame is made up of two thicknesses of timber) and wide enough to accommodate the curves of the finished shape. The blanks are glued and dowelled together. Then one rubber cements the tracing paper patterns to the wood blanks and commences to saw the frames to shape with a coping saw or jig saw.

8. One now turns to the assembly of the keel, stem and sternpost, the patterns for which are simply traced off the sheer plan. The stem and sternpost are "scarfed" to the keel with glue and dowels.

9. A baseboard is set up where a paper pattern is glued flat to it showing the exact location of each frame along the keel, and with end brackets and "keel blocks" contrived to keep the keel assembly upright and perfectly straight while the frames are fitted.

10. One next cuts out a "frame jig" from a piece of 1/8" masonite shaped to match the widest curve of the ship's waterlines. Notches are cut into the edges of the jig, each notch as wide as a frame, and spaced apart according to the frame positions. Two additional notches, fore and aft slip over the stem and sternpost to keep the jig in alignment. The jig is mounted on three or so blocks just high enough to match the height of its corresponding waterline and of a width equal to the "room" between the frames. The purpose of the jig is to provide sturdy, positive support for the frames while they are being fitted and glued to the keel.

BASEBOARD AND FRAME JIG

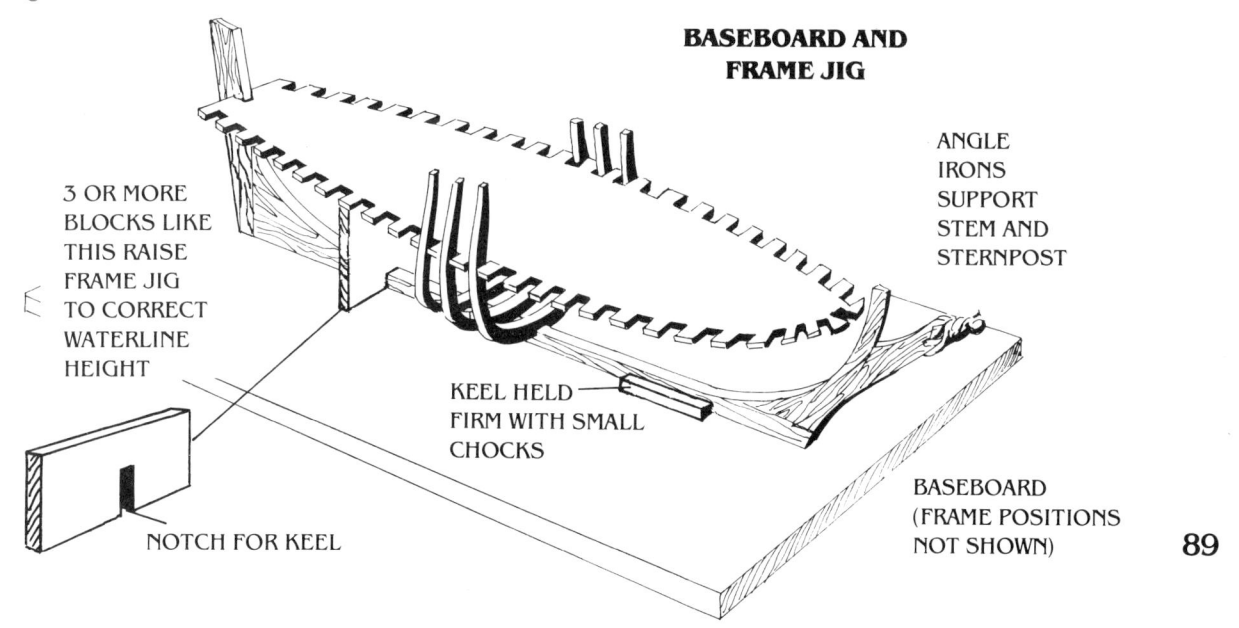

3 OR MORE BLOCKS LIKE THIS RAISE FRAME JIG TO CORRECT WATERLINE HEIGHT

ANGLE IRONS SUPPORT STEM AND STERNPOST

KEEL HELD FIRM WITH SMALL CHOCKS

NOTCH FOR KEEL

BASEBOARD (FRAME POSITIONS NOT SHOWN)

FRAME CONSTRUCTION

11. To assure myself that each frame will wind up in its exact position on the keel, I glue a 1/16" strip to the top of the keel, and saw notches into it.

12. The parts—each frame and the keel assembly—are now filed and sanded to their finished shapes. The frames must have their bevels filed in, and keel, stem and sternpost must have their rabbets. Finally, the faces of each frame will be given two coats of lacquer, well rubbed between coats.

13. The components are now assembled in the jig and the wales of the ship are fitted, then dowelled and glued to the frames. With the wales in place one removes the model from the jig and proceeds to the rest of the planking.

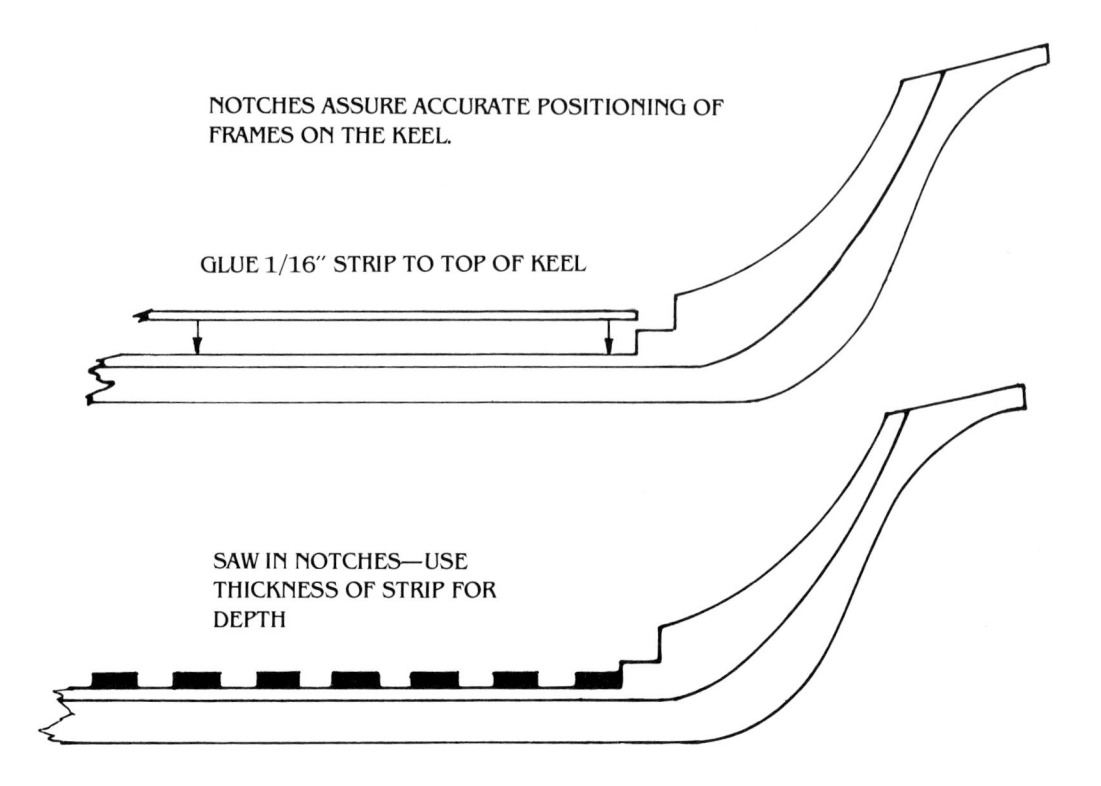

NOTCHES ASSURE ACCURATE POSITIONING OF FRAMES ON THE KEEL.

GLUE 1/16" STRIP TO TOP OF KEEL

SAW IN NOTCHES—USE THICKNESS OF STRIP FOR DEPTH

1. SIZE OF DOWELS—smaller the better. At 1/4" scale I use a #69 dowel, and a #68 drill.

2. FASTENINGS—one dowel for planks 8" wide or less. Planks 9" to 11" wide use two to every other rib, and one between. Planks 11" or more wide use two at each rib. I use two dowels at each rib for 9" planks for secure fastenings. (Davis says four dowels at each rib, but at 1/4" scale it can become very crowded.)

3. SIZE AND NUMBER OF PLANKS NEEDED between the bottom of the wale and the keel rabbet. Measure this distance at miship with a paper strip placed on the surface of the rib. Divide this distance by the number of planks you have decided to use to obtain rational width of plank stock. This should be about nine inches in scale. The planks will become a little wider at the stern, and slightly smaller at the stem. but the planks should not exceed much over 12" in width anywhere. If they come out too wide on the first go, increase the number of planks, and divide again.

4. RUN OF THE PLANKING. Use 1/16" square battens. Pin the first batten to the midship frame at the turn of the bilge, and let it follow the natural sweep of the hull, making contact with each frame; then pin it to every other rib. Now run another batten between the first batten and the keel, and another between the first batten and the under side of the wale. Use at least three battens on a 1/4" scale model. Be sure the battens run fair on the hull. Drill holes in the battens for the pins to prevent splitting. Use one of the pins for a drill bit. I also add a small touch of glue here and there to hold the pinned battens in place.

5. PLANK WIDTHS. Keep the planks to a maximum length of about 25 feet in scale as in real ship construction. The advantage in doing so is great. The short lengths can be bent by hand to fit the curve of the hull in most places, and you will not have to force bend curves across the width to fit the sheer curves.

PLANKING TIPS

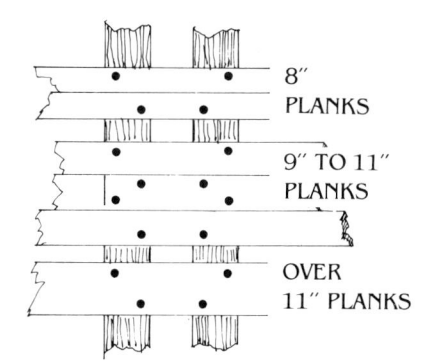

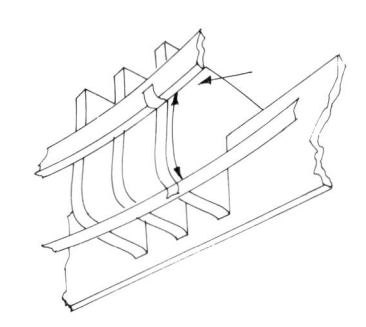

8" PLANKS
9" TO 11" PLANKS
OVER 11" PLANKS

USE A PAPER STRIP TO MEASURE DISTANCES AROUND FRAMES

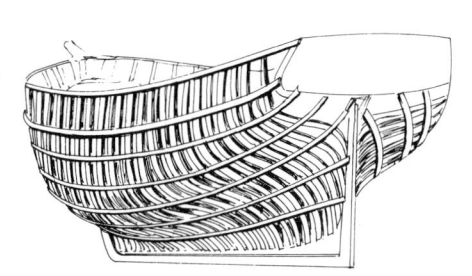

USE SPILING BATTENS TO ASSURE A FAIR RUN OF PLANKING

PLANKING TIPS

6. SPACING OF BUTT JOINTS. 3 strakes between joints on the same frame or rib; 5 feet between joints on adjoining strakes: 4 feet between joints with one strake between. Make a simple sketch showing the location of each butt joint. Just draw horizontal lines numbered for each plank, and numbered vertical lines for each rib. This method will make cutting the planks to the proper lengths a simple job, and will avoid any error.

7. SET YOUR PROPORTIONAL DIVIDERS for the number of planks needed between battens. Fit the first plank to the under side of the wale and cut it to fit the stem rabbet. Mark a vertical line on the plank at the center of each rib. Use the dividers to measure the width of the plank at the center of each rib holding the dividers with one point pressing slightly into the plank making a small dent. Do this at each rib, and then connect the points or dots with a straight edge using a fine pointed 6H pencil. Sand the edge to the finish line, and glue and dowel the plank into place. Work from the wale down, and the garboard strake up, and finish out the planking in the middle. This is the easiest place to fit the last plank run as the planks are nearly all the same width. Bevel the planks slightly at the curved section of the stem and stern to prevent a gap appearing between the strakes.

8. I use a piece of damp thick paper pressed over the last space for the final plank which, when the paper is dry it makes a perfect template.

9. Use small pins to hold ammonia-treated curved planks in place until they dry out. Be sure the pin holes correspond to the dowel holes to be drilled later on.

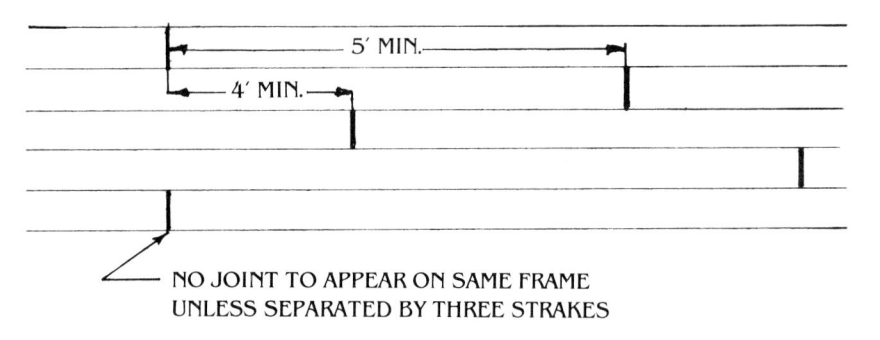

JOINTS SEPARATED BY ONE STRAKE AT LEAST 4' DISTANT

JOINTS OF ADJACENT STRAKES AT LEAST 5' DISTANT

NO JOINT TO APPEAR ON SAME FRAME UNLESS SEPARATED BY THREE STRAKES

An accurate method of working thin planks to the correct thickness is to use a Dremel Moto Tool and drill press. First saw out a supply of planks or timbers slightly thicker than the intended size. Make a small, hardwood "fence" and bolt it in place with wing nuts on the drill press table. Select a 1/4" or a 5/16" Dremel cutter or router. Insert it in the drill chuck and adjust the drill press table so that the space between the cutter and the table is exactly that of the desired finished plank.

Draw the timber toward you while holding it securely against the fence, and the cutter will plane the wood to the precise thickness. Use lower motor speeds with hard woods to avoid scorching of the material.

MACHINING TIMBER

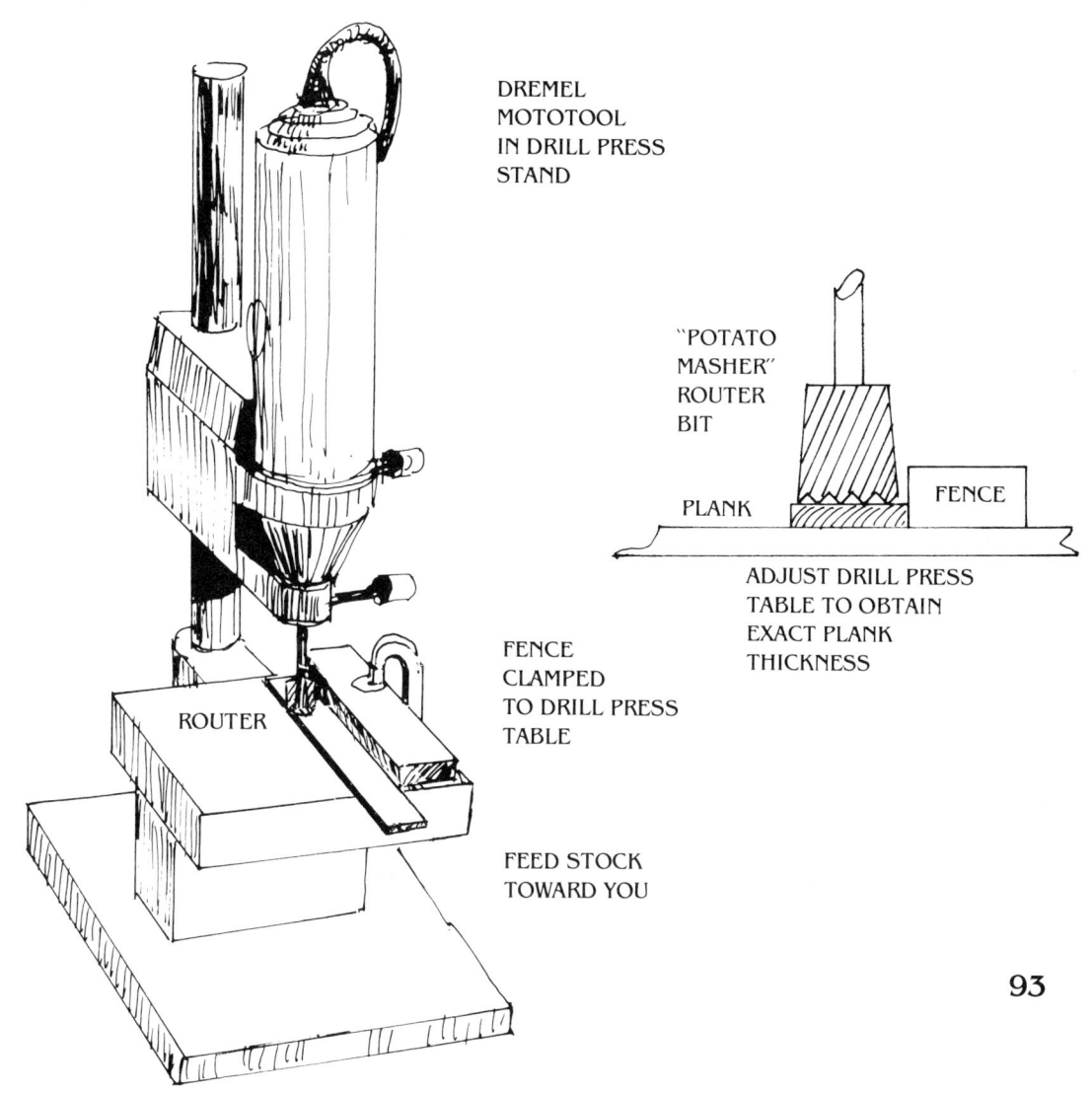

BAMBOO DOWELS

IRON OR STEEL DRAWPLATE WITH GRADUATED HOLES

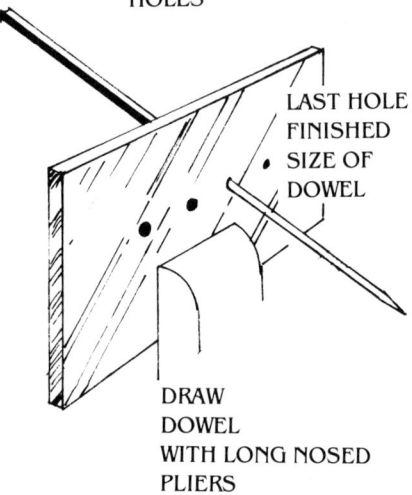

LAST HOLE FINISHED SIZE OF DOWEL

DRAW DOWEL WITH LONG NOSED PLIERS

Bamboo dowels make excellent fastenings in ship model construction. They can be sanded flush with planking, are strong, won't rust, and unlike metal fastenings, can be sawn through should they get in the way during the model's contruction

My sources of bamboo have been place mats, bamboo skewers and chopsticks, and finally a waste basket. Other sources are bamboo lawn rakes, old fishing poles, and of course the bamboo stalks themselves if they grow in your back yard.

Split 1/16" strips with a sharp knife, then soak them in a container of water. Soaked strips will pull through the draw plate easier, and when they dry out they will be a hair smaller in diameter. Point the ends of the strips.

Make a draw plate from a small piece of iron or steel 1/32" to 3/64" thick. Drill a series of holes in the metal, each hole becoming progressively smaller in diameter. The final hole will be the size of the dowel you have selected to use. My plate has four holes, the largest 1/16", and the other three made with #62, #69, and #74 drills. Drill #69 is just under 1/32" and #74 drill is just a little larger than 1/64". These two dowel sizes work best for me. Leave the burrs on the metal of the draw plate. They will increase its cutting capability.

Mount the draw plate securely in a vise. Insert the pointed bamboo into the 1/16" hole in the plate from the *burred* side. Grasp the bamboo point firmly with long nosed pliers and pull with a quick, sharp tug. The bamboo will peel off and a round 1/16" dowel will be formed. Point the dowel again and repeat the process in the rest of the holes until the desired dowel size is reached.

The holes drilled in the model should be one size larger than the dowel. Use a #73 drill for the #74 dowel, and a #68 drill for the #69 dowel, and so forth. This will permit easy insertion of the dowel, and allow for the thin glue in which the dowel has been dipped to set. A small, sharp point on the dowel will make it easy to start. Whenever possible the dowel holes should be drilled all the way through the wood in the model, and the dowel driven clear through to get the strongest fastening.

After the dowels are seated, clip off the ends as close as possible to the wood, then smooth the ends down flush with a fine file and sandpaper.

BUILDING OVER A MOLD

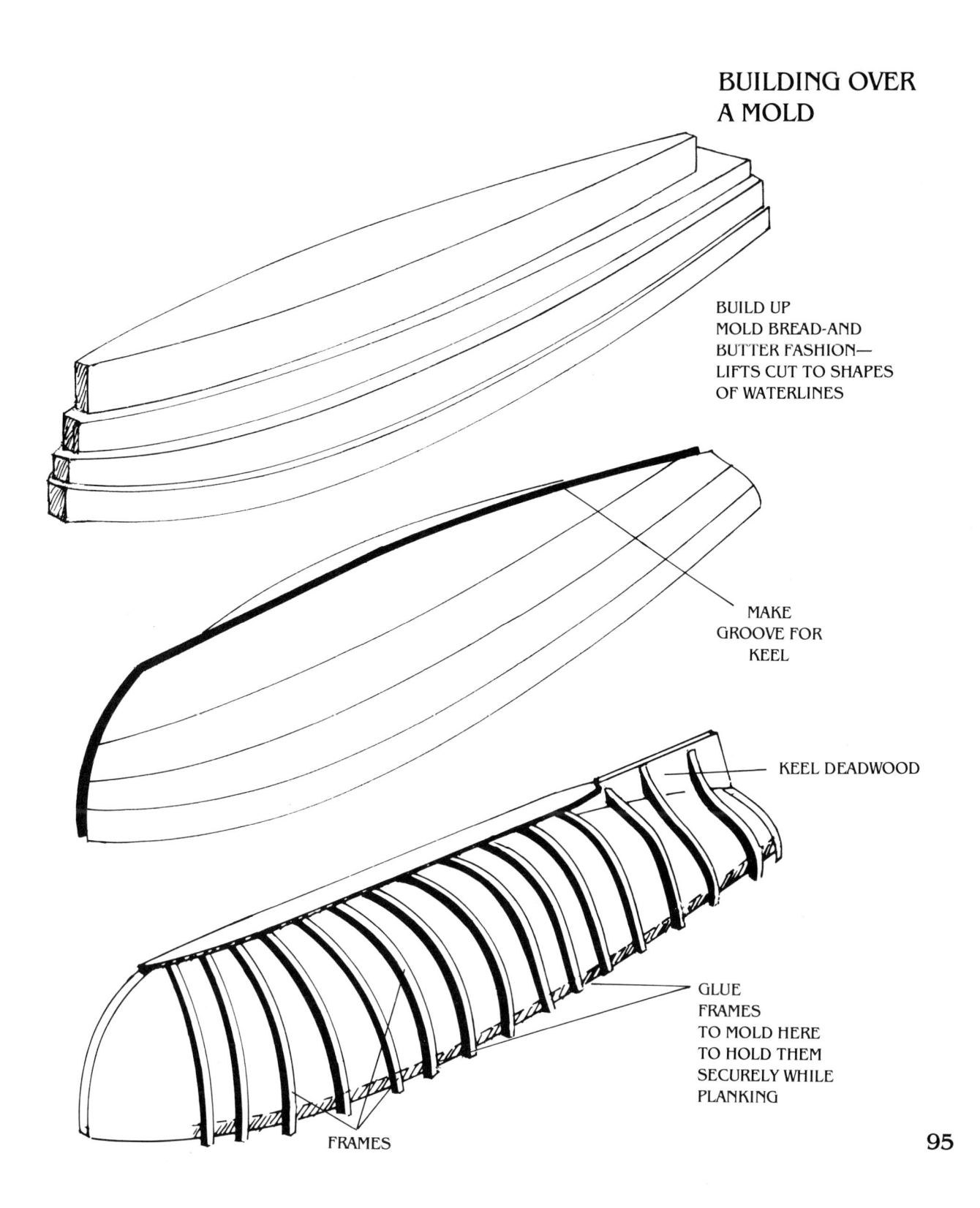

BUILD UP MOLD BREAD-AND BUTTER FASHION— LIFTS CUT TO SHAPES OF WATERLINES

MAKE GROOVE FOR KEEL

KEEL DEADWOOD

GLUE FRAMES TO MOLD HERE TO HOLD THEM SECURELY WHILE PLANKING

FRAMES

PINTLES AND GUDGEONS

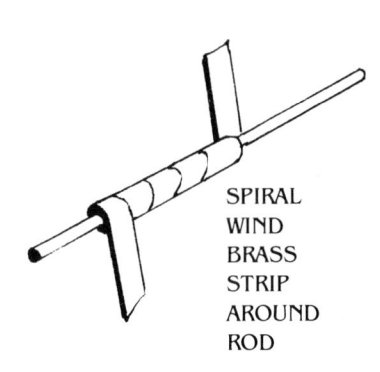

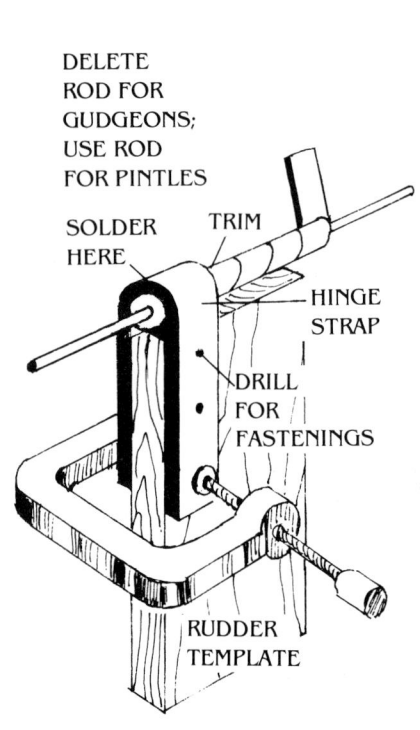

Here is a fairly easy way I've discovered to make rudder hardware. I used .007" and .010" sheet brass, and 1/32" brass rod for my 1/4" scale models. Other sizes apply to other scales.

1. Cut the .007" brass into a short strip 2 or 3 inches long, and 1/16" to 3/32" wide.

2. Wind the brass strip in a tight spiral around the 1/32" brass rod at about a 30 deg. angle–something like a stripe on a barber pole. Remove the rod and you have a short thin brass tube.

3. Cut a strip of .010" brass 1/16" or less wide which will be used for rudder "hinges."

4. Make two hardwood templates the exact thickness of the rudder, and of the sternpost.

5. Touch a very small part of the brass tube at the end with liquid solder paste, or tin it with a soldering iron. Keep the solder out of the tube hole.

6. Cut a 1" strip of .010" brass "hinge" stock, and put a dot of solder paste in the center, or tin a tiny spot with a small amount of solder.

7. *Pintle construction:* Put some solder paste on the tip of the 1/32" brass rod. Insert the rod into the tube about 3/32", and cut it off about 1/8" beyond the end of the tube.

8. Place the tinned brass tube with the inserted brass rod lengthwise on the edge of the rudder template. Bend the tinned "hinge" strap over the brass tube, and hold it in place with a clothespin clamp. Apply the soldering iron to the whole assembly for a moment. Cut off the tube flush with the "hinge" strap with a jeweler's saw and the pintle is done. (Fig. 2)

9. *Gudgeon construction:* Follow steps 1 through 6, and 8 using the *sternpost* template, and omit the brass rod. The gudgeon and pintle will fit perfectly.

RUDDERS

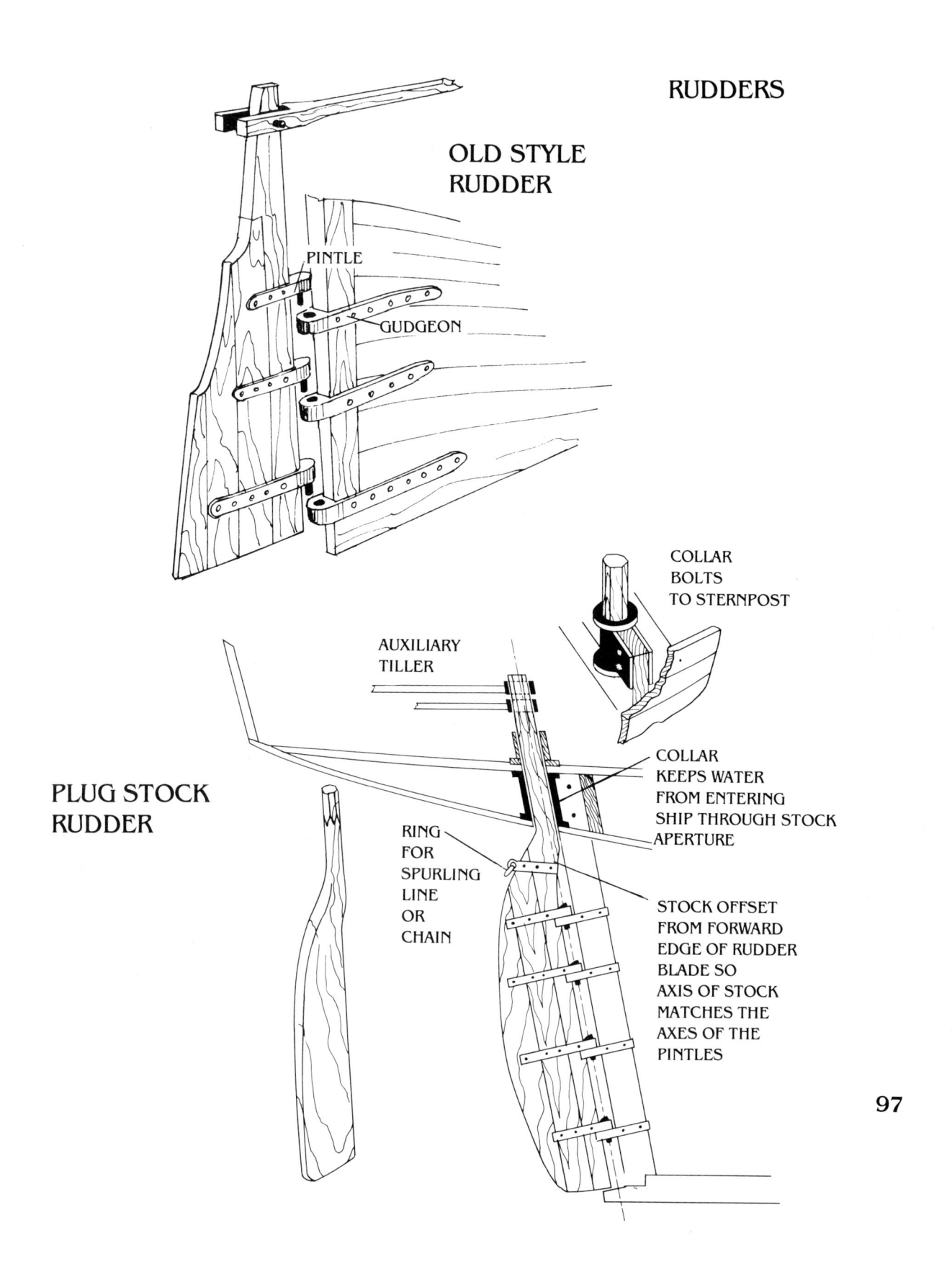

OLD STYLE RUDDER

PINTLE

GUDGEON

PLUG STOCK RUDDER

AUXILIARY TILLER

COLLAR BOLTS TO STERNPOST

COLLAR KEEPS WATER FROM ENTERING SHIP THROUGH STOCK APERTURE

RING FOR SPURLING LINE OR CHAIN

STOCK OFFSET FROM FORWARD EDGE OF RUDDER BLADE SO AXIS OF STOCK MATCHES THE AXES OF THE PINTLES

97

BELAYING PINS

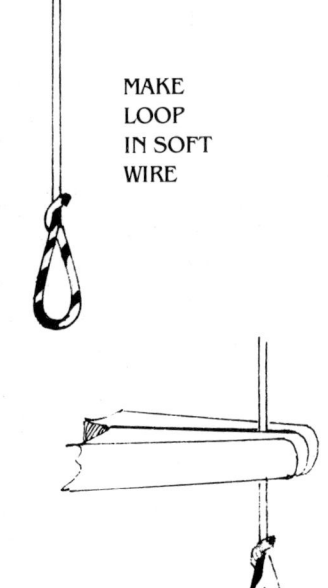

I wanted to buy them, but was unable to find belaying pins small enough in diameter to fit my need so I made some of copper wire. I made seventy-five.

I cut 3/4" lengths of 24 ga. copper wire, and bent one end 1/6" back on itself, forming a flat loop. Then I floated solder into the loop, holding the wire in a vertical position with a clothespin clamp. (Fig.2). The solder formed a teardrop shape as it melted and retained the shape when it cooled.

I chucked the straight end of the wire into my Dremel Moto Tool and started it spinning. I gently pressed the edge of the "teardrop" with a fine needle file until the blurring disappeared, after which I gave the "teardrop" the shape of a belaying pin handle with a half-round needle file. I finished my pins with a touch of flat black paint.

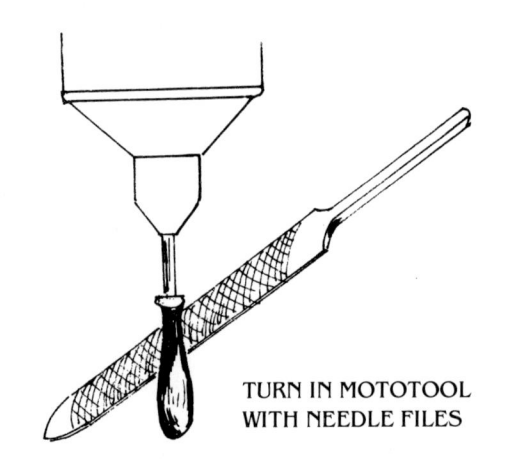

MAKE LOOP IN SOFT WIRE

TEARDROP OF SOLDER

TURN IN MOTOTOOL WITH NEEDLE FILES

BRASS BLOCK SHEAVES

1/16" 3/32" 1/8" 5/32"

Take a length of 1/16" diameter brass tubing, and with a small file make a slight groove around the circumference of the tube at one end. Slice off the grooved end the thickness of the sheave. The sheave is done, complete with a 1/32" hole in it for the sheave pin.

If you need a smaller hole, fill the tube with solder and redrill it to the smaller size.

Brass tubing diameters increase in 1/32" steps. A 1/16" tube slides into a 3/32" tube which slides into a 1/8" tube, and that tube fits into a 5/32" tube which is about as large a sheave as you could want.

To do this you need a small lathe with a face plate. Select a piece of boxwood, Swiss pear, birch or maple. Cut out a piece about 5/16" thick and 1¼" square. Glue one surface to a piece of heavy paper, and then glue the paper side to the surface of the lathe face plate. With a parting tool cut the outside and inside diameters of the wheel to a depth of about 1/8". Then cut the outside diameter of the wheel hub. Remove the wood between the inside of the wheel rim and the hub to a 1/8" depth. Cut some concentric grooves on the rim face for decoration, and drill a fine center hole in the hub for the wheel axle. Remove the wood from the outside of the wheel rim to about 3/16" depth.

Take the face plate off the lathe, and with a protractor mark off the divisions for the spoke holes on the ouside wheel rim. Line up the hub spoke holes with the marks using a straight edge.

Put the face plate back on the lathe. With a 1/32" drill, bore one hole carefully through the edge of the rim, the hub, and on through the rim again. Fit a brass rod through this set of holes to maintain alignment. Drill the balance of the spoke holes, but do not drill all the way through the hub on these. You would drill away the whole hub.

Make the wheel spokes with a Dremel Mototool. Fit a 3/4" length of 1/16" square boxwood into the chuck. Make a turning template out of a hacksaw blade cut to the profile of a spoke, then turn out as many matched spokes as you need.

Fit and glue the spokes into the holes in the rim/hub assembly, saving the holes with the alignment rod for last.

After the glue has set, gently remove the assembled wheel from the wood stock with a very fine toothed saw, sand and finish.

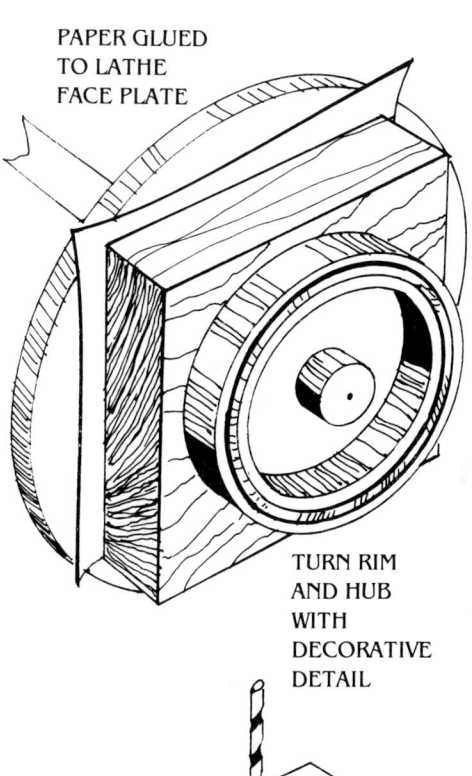

A SHIP'S WHEEL

PAPER GLUED TO LATHE FACE PLATE

TURN RIM AND HUB WITH DECORATIVE DETAIL

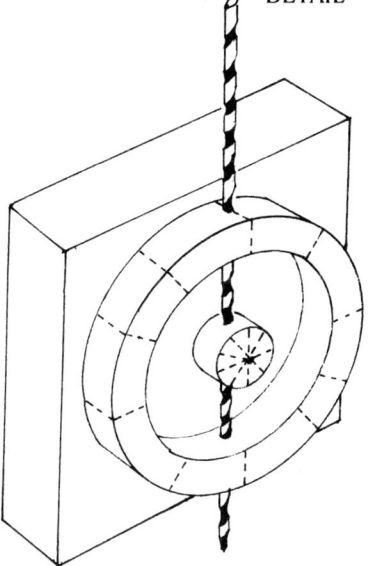

DRILL ONE SPOKE HOLE CLEAR THROUGH RIM HUB AND OPPOSITE RIM. DRILL OTHER SPOKE HOLES THROUGH RIM TO PARTIAL HOLE IN HUB

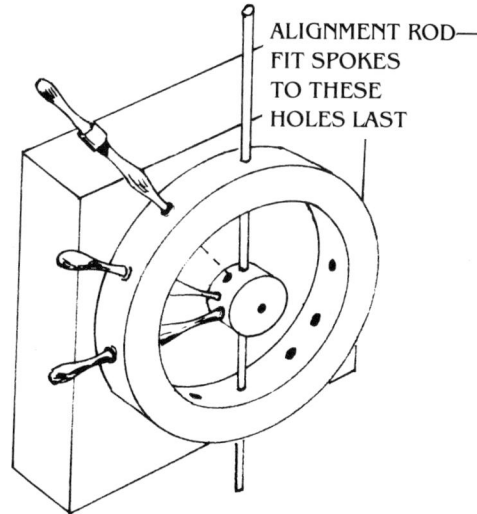

TURN SPOKES IN MOTOTOOL

FIT TO WHEEL

SAW WHEEL FROM BLOCK

ALIGNMENT ROD— FIT SPOKES TO THESE HOLES LAST

HATCH COVER OPEN

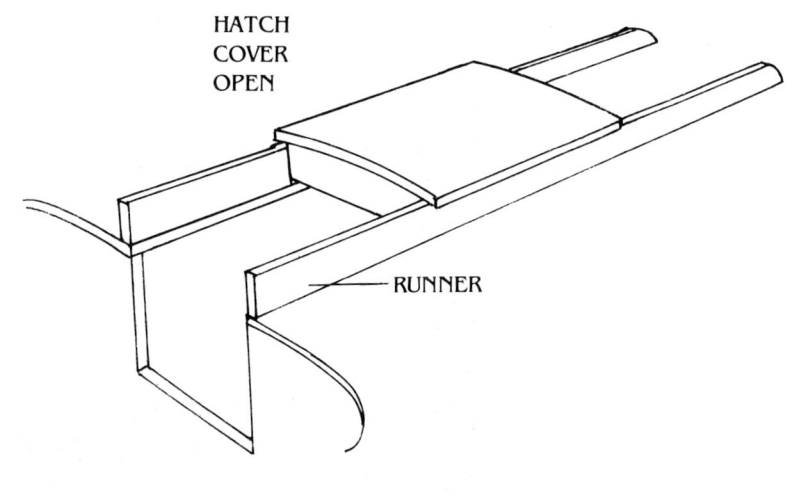

RUNNER

SLIDING COMPANION-WAY HATCH COVER

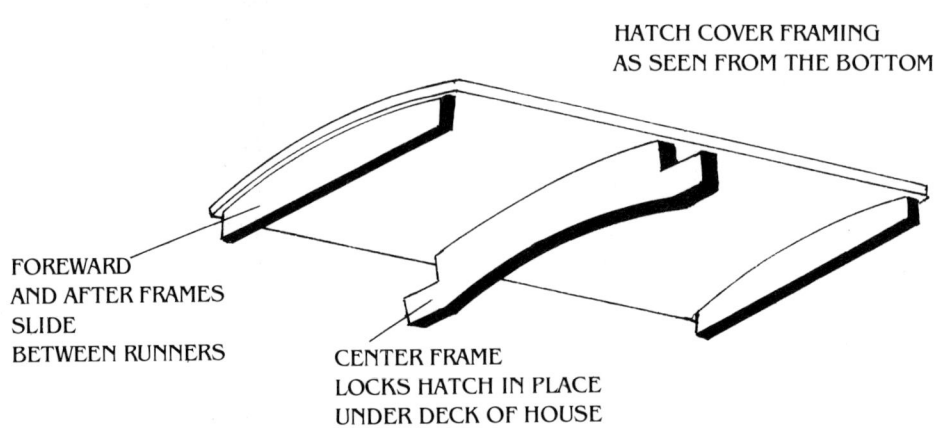

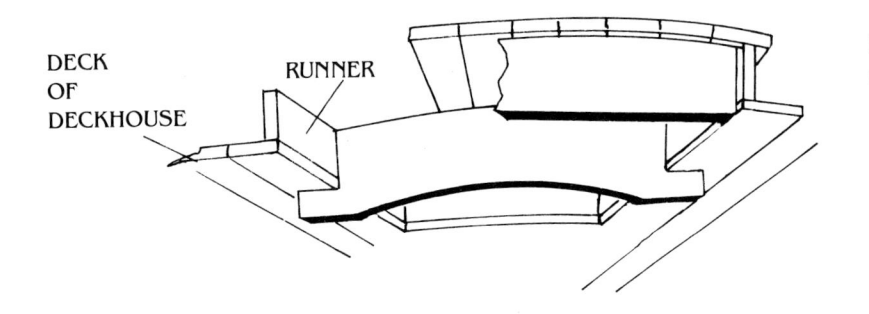

HATCH COVER FRAMING AS SEEN FROM THE BOTTOM

FOREWARD AND AFTER FRAMES SLIDE BETWEEN RUNNERS

CENTER FRAME LOCKS HATCH IN PLACE UNDER DECK OF HOUSE

DECK OF DECKHOUSE

RUNNER

FIT THE HATCH COVER TO THE DECKHOUSE BEFORE FASTENING THE DECKHOUSE TO THE DECK

Cut a strip of brass about two inches long and the width and thickness of the fluke. Tin one end with solder as well as the surfaces of the top ends of the arms where the flukes are to be fastened. Hold the tinned brass strip to a tinned arm, and sweat the parts together with a soldering iron. Cut off the strip at the tips of the arms and file the flukes to shape.

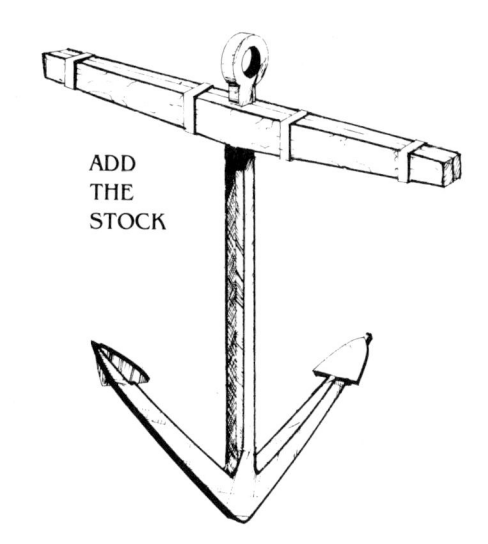

ANCHORS

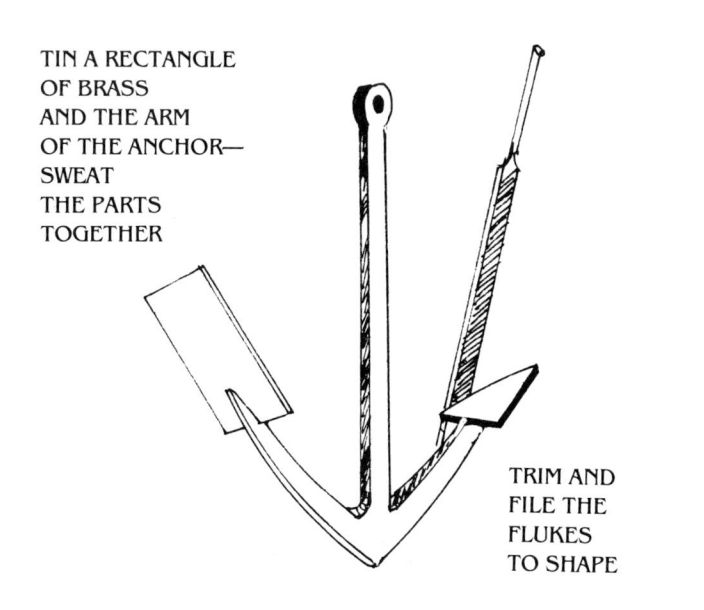

TIN A RECTANGLE OF BRASS AND THE ARM OF THE ANCHOR—SWEAT THE PARTS TOGETHER

TRIM AND FILE THE FLUKES TO SHAPE

ADD THE STOCK

BLACKEN BRASS AND OTHER METALS WITHOUT PAINT

After trying several chemical mixtures for blackshine metals with varying success I found Birchwood Casey metal blackening products to be the best. Their "Aluminum Black Metal Touch-up" will blacken brass or aluminum, and "Gunsmith's Magic Bluer" will blacken iron or steel nicely.

DEADEYES

GROOVE MARK OFF AND SAW BLANKS

Use boxwood, Swiss pear, or walnut. Turn the stock to the desired diameter on a small lathe, or with an electric drill. Mark off the thickness of each deadeye, then cut in the grooves for the shrouds between the marks. Slice off the discs at each mark to make yourself a supply of undrilled deadeyes. I use a pattern maker's file for cutting the grooves, and a fine bladed Exacto saw for slicing.

Make a drilling jig out of a small block of hardwood. Drill a hole the diameter of the deadeyes to a depth of the thickness of two deadeyes. Drill a smaller hole clear through the center of the hole in the jig block.

Take one blank deadeye and drill the three lanyard holes required. Insert a blank deadeye into the hole in the block. Place the drilled deadeye on top of it and use it as a pattern for drilling the holes in the blank underneath. After drilling the second set of lanyard holes, poke a toothpick through the hole in the bottom of the block and pop out both deadeyes.

Follow the procedure for the rest of your deadeyes and all the lanyard holes will be equally spaced.

Finish off the surfaces of the deadeyes by wrapping a piece of soft copper wire around the groove and giving it a twist or two. This will provide a secure vise for holding the deadeye while filing and finishing its face curves.

MAKE JIG WITH HOLE THICKNESS OF 2 DEADEYES

DRILL SMALLER HOLE THROUGH BOTTOM OF JIG

DRILL ONE DEADEYE FOR HOLE PATTERNS

USE SOFT WIRE FOR HOLDER

CHAINPLATES

Making chain plates to scale, yet strong enough to withstand the tension of the shrouds, can be a problem for the scratchbuilder. Here is a method I have developed which does a satisfactory job without sacrificing realism. I use soft iron wire because it can be blued to give the appearance of old ironwork.

CHAIN PLATES (CONTINUED)

There are three links required on a large number of ships. There's the upper deadeye strap, a middle or long link, and a bottom or toe link. (Fig. 1)

The deadeye strap is the most complex one to make. I made a simple jig consisting of a small block of hardwood, a drill the exact diameter of the deadeye being used, and a small brad the diameter of the iron wire being used for the strap.

I drilled a hole near one end of the block with the "deadeye" drill and left the drill in the block with the smooth shank exposed. I drove a brad into the block the exact distance from the drill that represents the lower end of the strap. I cut off the brad head and filed it smooth. (Fig. 2)

I flattened about 3/32" of the end of a short length of wire in a vise. Then with a long nosed pliers I wrapped the wire around my drill and brad jig and cut off the wire allowing a 3/32" overlap of its two ends. I flattened the second end to make a nice joint with the first. The first link became the pattern for the lengths of wire needed for all the other links. I used my jig to form the links, then soldered their ends.

I followed a similar procedure for the toe link and middle link, making a jig for each.

I soldered the ends of the middle link together when the other two links were in place on the chain.

3/32"
LAP JOINTS

DEADEYE LINK   LONG LINK   TOE LINK

THE CHAINS OF MANY SHIPS CONSISTED OF THREE LINKS SHAPED LIKE THIS

FIG. 1

JIG FOR MAKING CHAIN LINKS

USE DRILL OR NAIL OF CORRECT DIAMETER FOR MANDRELS

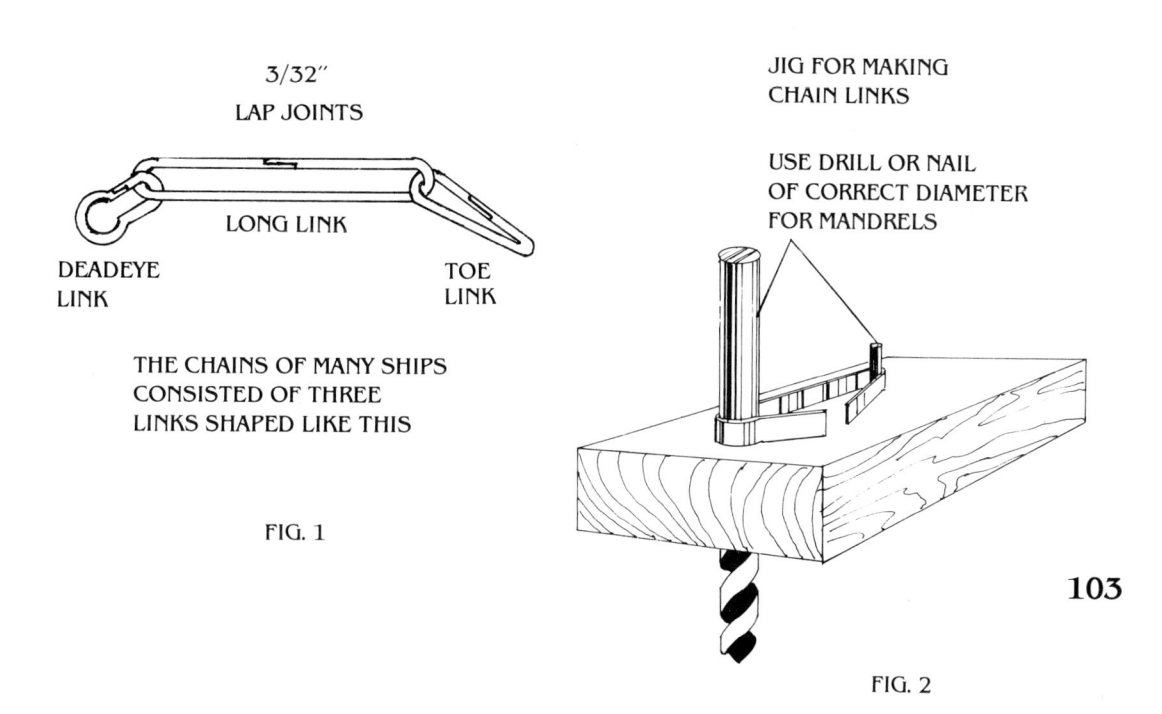

FIG. 2

BRASS OARLOCKS

Brass oarlocks for a ship's boats are easily made from brass tubing and wire. For a 1/4"=1'–0" scale small boat I selected a short length of 3/64" brass tubing. I filed it flat on one side until the tube's cross section resembled a partly closed U. At intervals of 3/64" along the sliced off tube I drilled 1/64" holes through the base of the U, then sawed off segments about 1/32" wide with a jeweler's saw. I inserted short lengths of 1/64" brass rod into the holes from the underside of the U and soldered them in place. I then finished my oarlocks with needle files.

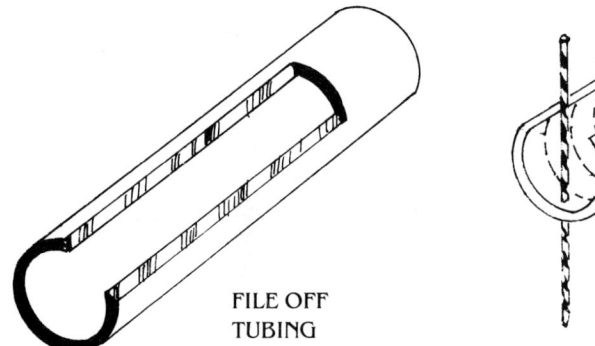

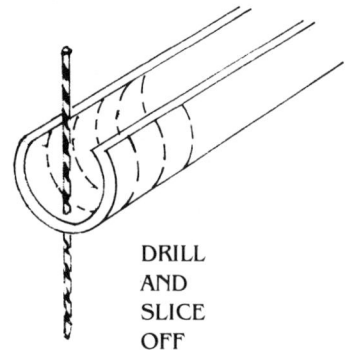

FILE OFF TUBING

DRILL AND SLICE OFF

SOLDER ROD IN HOLE

FINISH OARLOCK

MAST HOOPS

"Wooden" mast hoops used to fasten a fore and aft sail to the mast are hard to find in just the right diameter and thickness. I made satisfactory hoops of brown paper.

Cut brown paper strips about 2 inches wide and a foot long. Find a wooden dowel slightly larger than the diameter of the mast. A dowel can be made larger in diameter by wrapping and gluing paper around it.

Coat the surface of the dowel with several coats of Deft, and when it is dry give it a good coat of wax. Wrap the paper strip one turn around the dowel, and apply white glue to the surface with a small brush. Continue wrapping and gluing until the mast ring is thick enough.

When thoroughly dry, slice off the hoops with a sharp knife as you slowly rotate the dowel. If you did a good wax job on the dowel the rings will slide off easily.

Finish the hoops with two or three coats of Deft. They will look like they are made of wood.

MEASURE ROPE DIAMETERS

Wax a rope sample and wrap it a number of turns around a graduated steel rule. Keep the turns as close together as possible without flattening the rope.

Count the number of turns in one quarter of an inch on the rule and multiply by 4 to get the number of turns per inch. The number of turns per inch yields the diameter of the line. For example, 64 turns per inch means the line is 1/64" in diameter. In 1/4"=1'–0" scale, such a line would be the equivalent of a 3/4" diameter rope.

I have checked this method with my micrometer, and it is accurate to within 10%. A very fine thread can be measured this way. It is best to make two or three "test runs" to obtain an average measurement.

STOPPER KNOTS

Here is a simple, easy method my wife taught me for tying "stopper" knots when installing reef ropes on sails. The knots snug up where you want them without undesirable slack.

Tie a "stopper" knot on your reef rope, and pull the rope through the sail with a needle. Press the needle point tightly against the sail where the rope comes through. Make one or two loops around the needle point, and press the needle point against the knot on the opposite side of the sail. Hold it there with your thumbnail as you pull the needle through the loops, making a snug knot.

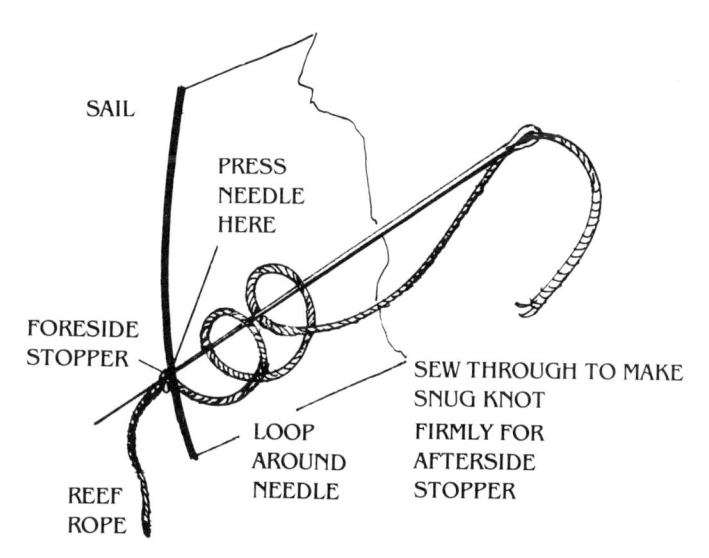

MODEL SAIL TABLING

Fastening a "hem" on the edges of a sail can be a chore. Here is an effective method I have worked out.

1. Draw the outline of the sail on very thin paper leaving a half inch or so border. Also draw the vertical lines indicating the sail cloth strips.

2. Pin the pattern to the material with the sail cloth strip lines running parallel to the selvage.

3. Have your wife (girlfriend) set her sewing machine to its finest stitch and ask her to stitch all of the lines drawn on the pattern into the sail cloth.

4. Carefully remove the pattern from the cloth. Then, allowing for the width of the sail hem, cut the cloth parallel to the stitched outline of the sail.

5. Cut notches in the four corners of the sail hem so it will fold neatly. Using a flatiron, fold the edges of the sail to the stitched outline. This should form a permanent crease with the stitching right on the edge.

6. Take a strip of 3M double-sided tape and press it on the cloth hem. Slowly remove the paper backing from the tape leaving the glue on the cloth. Press the glued side down on the sail forming the hem. Run over the hem a couple of times with the iron to get a nice, smooth edge, and the job is done.

7. The stitched outline will be just right for fastening the bolt ropes when they are sewn to the edges of the sail.

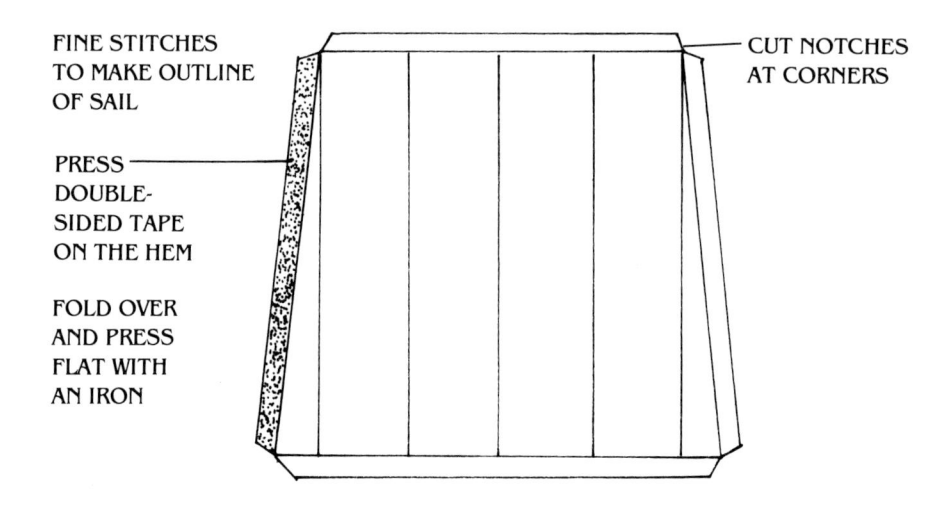

FINE STITCHES TO MAKE OUTLINE OF SAIL

CUT NOTCHES AT CORNERS

PRESS DOUBLE-SIDED TAPE ON THE HEM

FOLD OVER AND PRESS FLAT WITH AN IRON

TYPICAL SAIL LAYOUTS

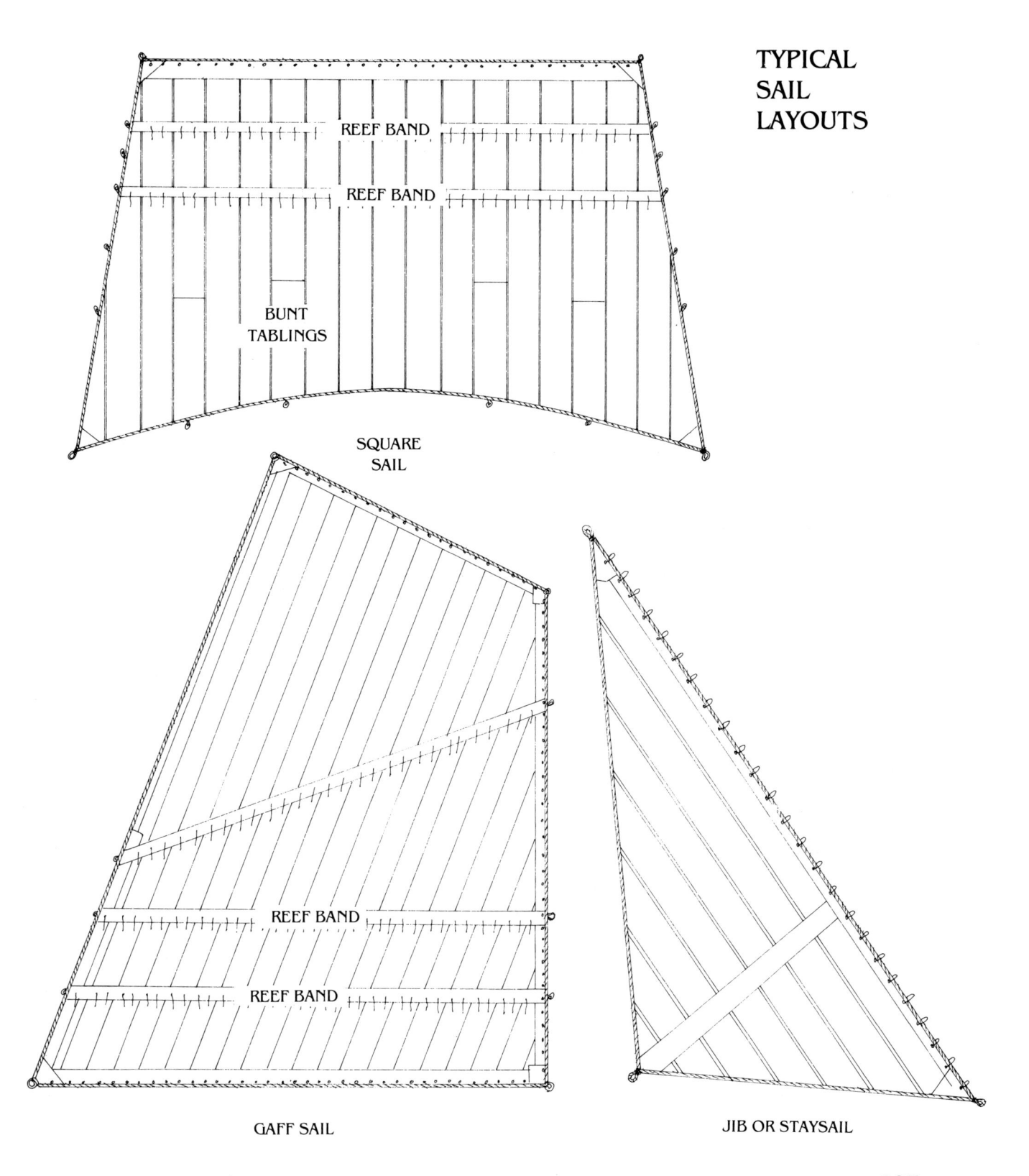

REEF BAND

REEF BAND

BUNT TABLINGS

SQUARE SAIL

REEF BAND

REEF BAND

GAFF SAIL

JIB OR STAYSAIL

MAKESHIFT TOOLS

Use discarded screw type earrings for small "C" clamps. (Check with your wife first!)

Use spring-type metal hair clips shaped to order, for heat sinks when doing multiple soldering jobs on small brass fittings.

Use a spring paper clip for holding thin wooden planks and beams while sanding and beveling them. Hold the item in the clamp and rub it over fine sandpaper placed on a flat surface. The trick gives you complete control without an unwanted manicure. I use clips that are, 1", 2½" and 3" long for different jobs.

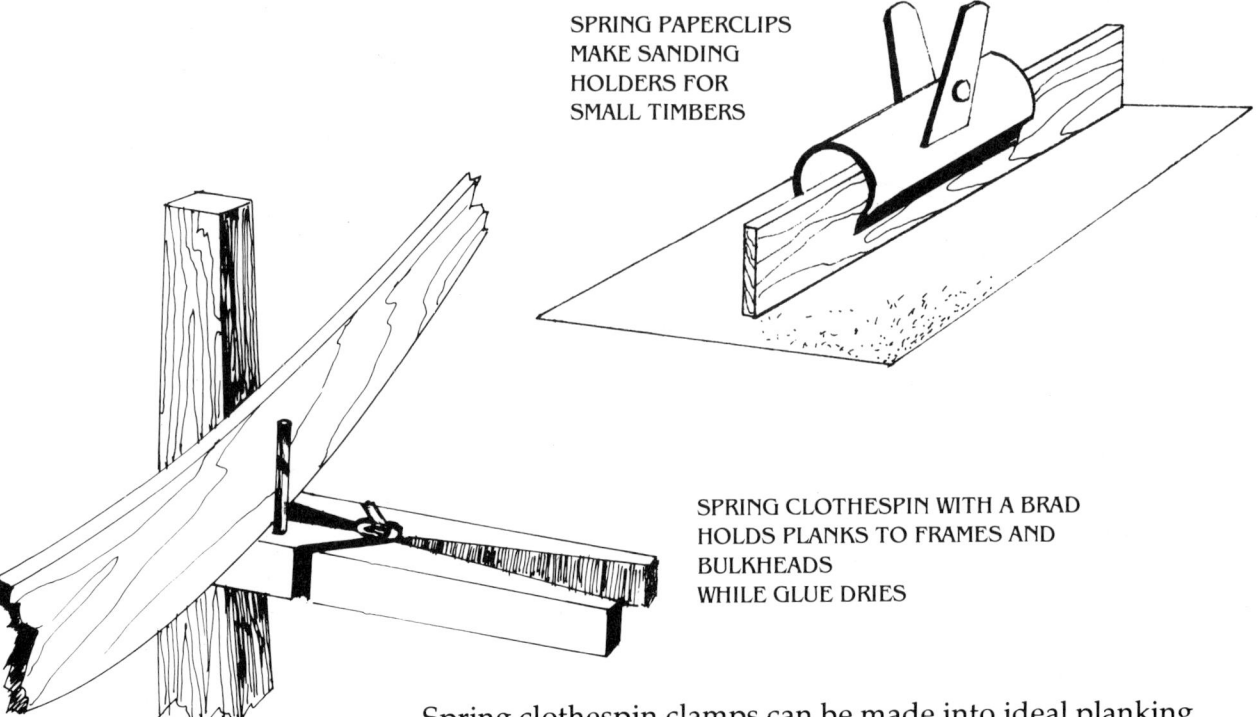

SPRING PAPERCLIPS MAKE SANDING HOLDERS FOR SMALL TIMBERS

SPRING CLOTHESPIN WITH A BRAD HOLDS PLANKS TO FRAMES AND BULKHEADS WHILE GLUE DRIES

Spring clothespin clamps can be made into ideal planking clamps. Drill a hole the size of a small brad or brass nail through the end of one jaw of the clamp, and about 3/4 inch from the end. Remove the head from the brad and insert it into the hole in the jaw. It should be a push fit, leaving about 1/4 inch exposed.

Let the clothespin grip the frames or bulkheads while the brad presses against the plank.

SMALL GRATINGS

Here is simple method I have used for making small gratings.

1. On a piece of tracing paper draw a series of 1/16 inch squares covering a surface the size of the grating needed.
2. Provide a 1/16 inch thick piece of hardwood a little larger in area than the grating will be.
3. With rubber cement secure the tracing paper to the wooden strip keeping the drawing lined up with the grain of the wood.
4. Mark each intersection of the lines on the drawing with a sharp center punch.
5. With a 1/32" drill bore holes through the strip at each punch mark.
6. File the shaft of a wire brad into a 1/32 inch square cross section and sharpen its point.
7. Insert the blunt end of the brad into the end of a short 1/4-inch square wooden handle. Align the flattened sides of the squared brad parallel to the sides of the handle.
8. Press the squared pointed, brad into the 1/32 inch holes in the grating stock, keeping the squared holes parallel to each other. If neatly done your round holes will become the square holes of your grating. Sand and finish the part to size.

BRAD POINT FILED SQUARE IS TOOL FOR MAKING SMALL ROUND HOLES SQUARE

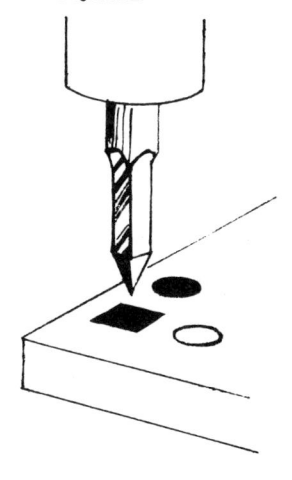

CURVED FILES

I found a use for a broken pattern-making mill file. The handle and about an inch of cutting surface remained, so I heated it until it was bright red in an open flame on the stove. I let it cool by itself and it became soft enough to file off the edges, and bend by hand over a one inch dowel. I used dowel because wood would not mar the softened cutting surface.

I rehardened the new-formed file by heating it again to a bright red, and dunking it in cold salt water.

I used this curved file for leveling off dowel heads on hull planking, getting at inside curves within the hull, and smoothing garboard strakes without scratching the keel.

When the file got dull, I reheated it, bent it the other way and took advantage of the other cutting edge.

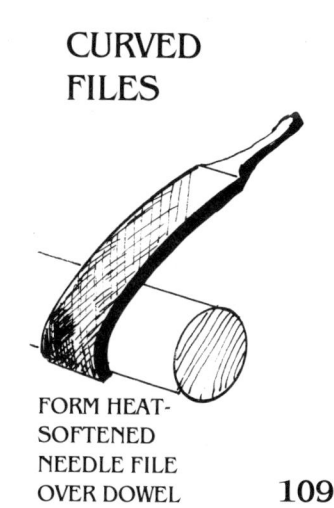

FORM HEAT-SOFTENED NEEDLE FILE OVER DOWEL

TOOL CHEST

Power Tools
- Dremel Moto Tool
- Scroll or jig saw
- Dremel speed control unit
- Bench saw with 7 inch hollow ground blade
- 4 inch power sanding disk
- Small wood turning lathe
- Dremel drill press
- Dremel 4 inch table saw

Hand tools
- Strong small vise on a ball socket
- Work bench
- Small metal miter box
- 3 and 6 inch try square
- Sharp three-bladed knife
- Wood carving tools
- Single edged safety razor blades
- Light weight hammer
- Long nosed pliers
- Flush cutting side cutter pliers
- 6 inch steel rule with 1/64 inch graduations
- Swiss pattern maker's files
- Fine cut metal file, medium cut rasp, small rattail file
- Soldering iron
- Coping saw
- Fine toothed back saw
- Small twist drills of various sizes, #61 through #80
- Pin vise for small drills
- Small C clamps
- A dozen or more wooden spring clothespins
- Bevel
- Protractor
- Center punch and a metal scriber
- Work Mate—8 inch bench vise
- Drill gauge sizes #61 through #80
- Jeweler's saw and blades
- 24 inch flexible curve ruler
- Copy Cat—6 inch metal curve copier

Dental picks and drills
Proportional dividers
Micrometer
Uber knives
Opti-Visor optical glass binocular magnifier

Drafting tools
Dividers, drawing compass, etc.
Drawing board
T square
Triangles—French curves
Architect's scale
6H pencils

SOURCES OF PLANS AND OTHER DATA

GENERAL
Underhill, Harold A.
Plank-on-Frame Models, Vol. 1
Glasgow, 1978

Davis, Charles G.
The Built-Up Ship Model
New York, 1933
Ship Modelers Association
Fullerton, CA

MALEK ADHEL
Popular Science Monthly
New York, N.Y.
March–June, 1937

A SPANISH GALLEON
Plans: Billing Boats, Denmark

THE SHIP FROM KYRENIA
National Geographic
Washington, D.C., November 1974

THE SHIP FROM YASSI ADA
Bass, G.
A History of Seafaring
London, 1972
Landstrom, B.
The Ship
Stockholm, 1961

A CARRACK OF THE 14TH CENTURY
Landstrom, B.
The Ship
Stockholm, 1961

THE SHIP FROM KALMAR
Bass, G.
A History of Seafaring
London, 1972
Landstrom, B.
The Ship
Stockholm, 1961

THE BRIG IRENE
Petrejos, E. W.
Irene, A Handbook for the Building of Historic Ship Models
Hengelo, Holland, 1970

THE THOLENSE HOOGARS TH64
Plans: van Betan, J.
Nautical Research Journal
6413 Dahlonega Road
Washington, D.C., 20016
June 1976

THE SAMBUC OF ARABIA
Plans: Lusci, V.
   Via Pescetti, 6 Firenze, Italy
Villiers, A.
Sons of Sinbad
New York, N.Y. 1960

A CHINESE WAR JUNK
Plans: Lusci, V.
Firenze, Italy

THE VIRGINIA OF THE SAGADAHOCK
Plans: Langbehn, C. M.
Nautical Research Journal
June 1977

A COLONIAL BARK
Plans: Baker, William A.
Boston, 1962

THE HANNAH
Plans: Chapelle, H and Edson, M.
of schooner *Sir Edward Hawke*
Nautical Research Journal

A TANCOOK WHALER
Plans: Chapelle, H.
American Small Sailing Craft
New York, N.Y. 1937

SPRAY, CAPTAIN SLOCUM'S SLOOP
Slocum, J.
Sailing Alone Around the World
New York, N.Y. 1898

A U.S. NAVY ANCHOR HOY
Plans: Grice, E.
in Grimwood, V. R.
American Ship Models
New York, N.Y. 1942

FANNY M
A PISCATAQUA RIVER GUNDALOW
Plans: Taylor, D. F.
in Grimwood, V. R.
American Ship Models
New York, N.Y. 1942